VALUES

H.A.B.I.T.S.

of spiritual growth

VALUES

&

HABITS

of spiritual growth

Bryan Gray

V.A.L.U.E.S. & H.A.B.I.T.S. *of spiritual growth*

ISBN: 978-0-9849087-6-9

About the author: Bryan Gray is an experienced teen, campus, singles and families minister. He is married to Rachel and they have three children (Grace, Ella and Parker). Bryan did his undergraduate work at Carnegie Mellon and Stony Brook University where he majored in Fine Arts and History.  Bryan is a fun-loving, energetic man who is passionate about teaching and preaching God's Word. You can find his latest articles, sermons and resources at *www.BryanGrayMinistries.com*. He would love to hear from you during your one-year journey. Please send suggestions, corrections and any additional ideas you have for this work. Bryan can be reached at his website.

Illumination Publishers International
www.ipibooks.com
6010 Pinecreek Ridge Court
Spring, Texas 77379-2513, USA

Dedication

To my wife Rachel,
for every unseen thing you do for Christ,
myself, our children and everyone else.

Contents

Contents

Contents

Acknowledgements

Lord, your love and grace has made me everything I am!

This book is dedicated to my wife Rachel. You truly are my best friend, a woman of God, an amazing sister in Christ and the one God uses to sharpen me the most. If it wasn't for you balancing my craziness I wouldn't be the man I am today. Finally, I want to thank you for following me across several states, churches and ministries as we've served God together.

A special thanks to Roger Wine who has probably spent as much time as my wife listening to me work out the thoughts and ideas found within these pages. Thank you for your constant love and friendship. You are my closest *haverim*.

A special thanks to all of the brothers in the New England churches who helped edit sections of this book.

In the final analysis, this book was a community project. So many brothers over the years have written quiet time series that have changed my life, and many of those thoughts and concepts are found within these pages. Your work is appreciated.

Introduction

*"If you possess these qualities in increasing measure...
you will never fall."* —2 Peter 1:5-10

This book isn't really about just having quiet times over the next few weeks, months and year. It's about the rest of your life! It's about when you breathe your last breath will you have fought the good fight, finished the race and kept the faith (2 Timothy 4:7).

In the end of the day it doesn't matter how graceful you looked while running with Christ. It doesn't matter how many times you stumbled and fell flat on your face (Proverbs 24:16). It doesn't matter how badly life's battles left you bruised, bleeding and gasping for breath. The only thing that matters at the end of the day is did you persevere? Did you decide that staying on the ground beaten was somehow safer or better than getting back up and staying in the fight against sin? Did you allow Satan to deceive you and harden your heart so much by the world's pleasures that you took your eyes off Christ and lost your hope in his eternal love? Or did you stay faithful?

If your goal is to stay faithful till the end (Mark 13:13), then make it your goal to never stop growing in Christ (2 Peter 1:5-11). For, *"if you possess these qualities in increasing measure... you will never fall."*

This book is centered around the goal of developing the qualities needed for life-long growth in Christ. This book is about the V.A.L.U.E.S. & H.A.B.I.T.S. of spiritual growth (see Diagram I on page 12).

The two acronyms above represent, 1) The things we need to do to grow and mature (H.A.B.I.T.S.), and 2) The heart and motivation behind each habit (V.A.L.U.E.S.). Your values and habits work together to remind you of what to do and why you do it.

If you lose the heart behind your habits eventually you will stop doing them. For example, many Christians break the habit of "A-ttending regular church meetings" because they lose the value that they "A-lways need encouragement to endure."

The basic goal of this book is, by the end of the year, to help you develop the V.A.L.U.E.S. & H.A.B.I.T.S. of spiritual growth. It's one year to consistently develop just 6 values and 6 habits. Remember, it's not about doing something fast it's about doing something that lasts. It's about remaining in the love of Jesus Christ from now into eternity!

Getting the Most from This Book

Today's Take Away: At the end of each day there will be one or two basic points to help you apply the day's lesson to your life. A quiet time with God really amounts to very little if you don't walk away with something that helps change you for the better.

A Verse To Remember: This is a Bible verse to memorize and meditate on. Transforming your life starts with changing the way you think and how you see the world. "*Be transformed by the renewing of your mind*" (Romans 12:2). Memorizing and meditating on scripture helps you replace your old way of thinking with a new godly way of thinking.

Discipleship Time: When you "U-nderstand my need for godly training" you will learn to "I-nvite discipling in my life." To help in this discipling relationship I wrote a *Discipleship Guide* that can found at the end of this book (page 122). The "*Discipleship Guide*" is designed for an older Christian to help you each week to discuss, digest and apply the lessons you've learned from that week. Spiritual growth happens best with the help of other brothers and sisters in Christ (Hebrews 10:24).

I pray this next year will help transform the rest of your life!

V.A.L.U.E.S. & H.A.B.I.T.S. (Diagram I)

(I)   (Therefore, I)

V-alue my relationship w/ God, above all. • **H**-ave a daily Quiet Time.

The greatest command in the Bible is to love God (Mark 12:30) above all (Matthew 10:37). That love is built by listening to him (2 Timothy 3:16), and speaking to Him (1 Thessalonians 5:17) everyday.

A-lways need encouragement to endure • **A**-ttend regular church meetings.

We are saved if we stay faithful till the end (Mark 13:13). That's why we must meet regularly to encourage one another (Hebrews 10:25), and to stay encouraged and faithful (Hebrews 3:13).

L-et God's Word guide my life. • **B**-iblically memorize and meditate.

Our ways lead to death (Proverbs 16:25), but God's ways lead to life. We change our ways by renewing our minds (Romans 12:2), and replacing our thoughts with God's thoughts (Psalms 119:11, 97-99).

U-nderstand my need for godly training. • **I**-nvite discipling in my life.

We all need to continually be taught and trained to obey God's commands (Matthew 28:20, 1 Timothy 4:7-8). This happens by "one another" relationships (Hebrews 3:23, 10:23), and learning from more mature disciples (Titus 2:3-7).

E-njoy bringing souls to Christ. • **T**-ell others the Good News.

When you love someone you want to give them what they want, and God wants all men to be saved (1 Timothy 2:4). That is the great commission God has given you (Matthew 28:19-20).

S-incerely meet the needs of others. • **S**-erve others with my S.H.A.P.E.

Becoming more like Christ means that we genuinely care about the needs of others (Philippians 2:3-4, 20). God has given you spiritual gifts (Romans 12:6-8) to serve and meet those needs (Galatians 6:10).

Day 1: 40 Days in the Desert

The first 40 days of any journey is the hardest. It's when you are the most vulnerable to lose focus, be discouraged and stop what you've started. If you can get through the first 40 days your chances of following through to the end will be much greater. Take a moment to begin today by asking God to give you the strength and discipline to finish what you've started.

Matthew 3:16-4:11
- What happened to Jesus after his baptism?
- What should you expect after baptism and your start today?
- What did Jesus use to fight Satan's temptations?

Psalm 119:11
- What is Psalm 119:11 instructing you to do and why?
- Satan's goal is to get you to fall into sin. Satan tried to get Jesus to sin, but Jesus kept quoting Scripture to him.

Ephesians 6:10-17
- From v. 11, what do you need to stand against?
- List some ways Satan may scheme against you this month.
- From v. 17, what is your "defense" weapon against Satan?

Acts 2:41-47
- After baptism what four things did they devote themselves to?
- Why do you think they devoted themselves to those things?

Today's Take Away
1. Over the next 40 days be on high alert for Satan's schemes.
2. Set a specific time and place to have your daily quiet time.
3. Plant Ephesians 6:11 deep in your heart today.

Day 2: *Growing Roots*

Luke 8:13

- What should you be rooted in (see Ephesians 3:16-19)?
- What happens to disciples who don't grow roots?

Ephesians 4:14

- It's important to have roots because what will try to blow you away?
- Do you want Satan to blow you away from God because you don't have deep roots?

Today's Take Away

1. There are a few central principles that the Bible teaches are essential for any disciple who wants to stay rooted in Christ till the end. The following two acronyms are designed to make those principles easier for you to remember and to apply. Each acronym represents: What you do (H.A.B.I.T.S.), and 2) Why you do it (V.A.L.U.E.S.). Before we will do anything we must believe that 1.) I can actually do it, and 2.) It's really worth it. Therefore, the two acronyms work together to remind you, "It's definitely worth it, and I can do it."

2. Over the next 39 days you'll slowly learn these two acronyms and memorize one verse that goes along with each value and habit. Don't worry about memorizing them all at once. We'll spend a few days on each one individually.

3. For today just copy what you see in the diagram on the next page onto a note card and remind yourself that you want to start forming the new values and habits that will keep you rooted in God's love.

The V.A.L.U.E.S & H.A.B.I.T.S. of Spiritual Growth!

(I)

V-alue my relationship w/ God, above all.

A-lways need spiritual encouragement to endure.

L-et God's Word guide my life.

U-nderstand my need for godly training.

E-njoy bringing souls to Christ.

S-incerely care about the needs of others.

(Therefore, I)

H-ave a daily Quiet Time.

A-ttend regular church meetings.

B-iblically memorize and meditate.

I-nvite discipling in my life.

T-ell others the Good News.

S-erve others w/ my S.H.A.P.E.

Possess these qualities in increasing measure...and you will never fall!

Day 3: *Loving God*

Mark 12:28-31
- What is the most important command/conviction in the entire Bible?
- What do you think it means to love God with:
  - All your HEART (your emotions)?
  - All your SOUL (your whole being)?
  - All your MIND (understanding)?
  - All your STRENGTH (efforts)?

Matthew 10:37-39
- Should you love anyone more than God?
- Should you put any relationship before yours with God?
- What happens if you love or put anyone before God?

James 4:8
- Does God want you to continue to draw closer to him?
- If you draw closer to God what will he do in return?
- How do you think you can get closer to God?
- How often should you take time to get closer to God?

Today's Take Away

1. We build relationships by communicating with one another. In the same way, you draw closer to God by listening to him through his Word and speaking to him in prayer. This is what a Quiet Time with God is all about.

2. Take an index card and write down the value, habit and two scriptures on the following page. Over the next several days take the index card with you everywhere you go and memorize and meditate on the statement and two scriptures.

(1) Value my relationship w/ God, above all. (Therefore, I) **Have a Daily Quiet Time.**

"Love the Lord your God with all your heart, soul, mind and strength."

– Mark 12:30

"Come near to God and he will come near to you."

– James 4:8

Day 4: *I Am a Christian But I Still Sin*

As a new Christian you will still have to deal with sin in your life. It will be a battle for you as long as you live. Every Christian needs to know that sin is real, even in the life of those who follow Jesus. Thank God that he deals with sin in a way that you can continue to walk in forgiveness.

1 John 1:5-10

- To have fellowship with your heavenly Father, what does he want you to practice daily (v. 6)?
- According to verse 7, in what must you walk or live?
- What does it practically mean to walk in the light?
- What does the blood of Jesus do for you when you walk in the light (v. 7)?
- In verse 9, what is required of you daily to be pleasing to God and to be assured he has forgiven you?

Today's Take Away

1. Know for sure God deeply loves you.

2. Know by walking in the light (God's truth) you are pleasing God.

3. Be willing each day to ask God to forgive you of those things that would displease him.

4. Ask God to help you to replace the bad habits in your life with the character traits of Jesus.

5. Continue memorizing and meditating on your first new value and habit.

Day 5: How Do I Pray?

Luke 11:1-13
- Why do you think prayer needs to be learned?
- From verse 2, who should we pray to?
- From verses 2-4, what four things should we pray for?
- From verses 5-13, what else should we know about prayer?

Philippians 4:6-7
- When you are stressed and worried, what should you do?
- And from verse 7, what will be the outcome?
- Do you feel at peace after you pray?

1 John 5:14
- If your prayers are in line with God's will, will God grant your request?
- Read 2 Corinthians 12:7-9.
- Paul made a request to God, but the answered was "No."
- Sometimes God answers with a "Yes, "No, or "Wait." Trust his answers, and don't be discouraged if he answers "No."

Ephesians 6:18-20
- What do you think it means to pray in the Spirit?
- Who and what should we be praying for?
- Do you pray for yourself (and for others in the kingdom) to be bold and effective in the sharing of the Gospel?
- A simple outline for prayer is: **A.C.T.S.**
  Adore, Confess, Thank, and Supplicate (make requests).

Today's Take Away

1. Pray using Luke 11:2-4 or the **A.C.T.S.** format.
2. Make a prayer journal and write down your prayer requests.
3. Continue memorizing and meditating on your first new value and habit.

Day 6: The Holy Spirit

Ephesians 2:18
* How does the Holy Spirit help us approach God?

Romans 8:2
* The Holy Spirit has freed us from what two laws?

Romans 8:26
* What does this scripture say about the help we receive from the Holy Spirit?
* What other action of the Holy Spirit do we see revealed in this scripture?

2 Corinthians 3:17
* According to this scripture, who is the Holy Spirit?
* According to this scripture, what does the Holy Spirit bring to the Christian?

Today's Take Away

1. Pray. Pray. Pray every day. God's Holy Spirit is there to help you.

2. Remember you may not know what to pray for or how to ask God. But His Holy Spirit is there to help you. _He wants to hear from you._

3. Continue memorizing and meditating on your first new value and habit.

Day 7: *God's Grace*

Ephesians 2:8-10

- From verse 8, how is "grace" defined?
- Did you earn your salvation?
- From verse 10, what does God's grace lead you to do?
- Read Romans 6:23.
  - As a sinner, what did you earn?
  - As a disciple, what gift did God give you through Jesus Christ?

Romans 5:6-11

- How did God prove his incredible love for you?
- From this passage, list the things Christ's death has done on your behalf.

Titus 2:11-14

- Has God's saving grace been teaching you to say "No!" to what is ungodly?
- Read Jude 1:4. What does false grace lead to?

1 Corinthians 15:9-10

- How did Paul show his gratitude towards the grace given him?
- How are you showing your gratitude towards the grace given you?

Today's Take Away

1. Write down (and do) three things that will express your gratitude towards God's grace.

2. Each day, show your appreciation of God's grace by doing what is good and pleasing in his sight.

3. Continue memorizing and meditating on your first new value and habit.

Day 8: *The Hope of Glory*

1 Corinthians 15:51-58
- What is the mystery Paul tells us?
- Why do people normally fear death?
- Why should we, as disciples, no longer fear death?
- Why should we devote ourselves fully to the work of the Lord?

Colossians 3:1-4
- Since you have been raised with Christ in baptism, what should you be thinking about from now on?
- What are some signs that indicate we are setting our minds on earthly things?
- How do you control what you are thinking about?

Hebrews 10:32-35
- Did these early disciples put their trust in the things of this world?
- How do we take a stand when we are going through suffering?
- Why did they joyfully accept the confiscation of their earthly possessions?

Today's Take Away

1. Think for a while about what heaven will be like. And don't forget to thank God every day for the opportunity to go to Heaven!

2. Continue memorizing and meditating on your first new value and habit.

Day 9: Family of God

God wants all of his children to stay faithful till the end (Mark 13:13), and he tells us that our best way of doing that is by sticking together (Hebrews 3:12-13). That is what the family of God is all about. It's about running the race, fighting the good fight and keeping the faith **together** (2 Timothy 4:7).

John 3:1-5
- When we are born physically what do we enter into?
- When we are "born again" spiritually what do we enter into?
- Do you view God's church as your spiritual family?

Mark 3:31-35
- Who did Jesus consider his true relatives?
- Do you see God's church as your spiritual family?

1 Peter 1:22-23
- What is sincere love?
- In what practical ways do you think you can love your brothers and sisters in Christ deeply from the heart?

Today's Take Away

1. Make it your goal this week to spend time with two or more Christians that you haven't fellowshipped with.

2. Honor the family of God and be devoted to the brotherhood of believers through phone calls, visits, emails, and fellowships.

3. Take an index card and write down the statement and two scriptures from the next page. Over the next several days take the index card with you everywhere you go and memorize the statement and the two scriptures.

(I) Always need spiritual encouragement to endure. (Therefore, I) Attend regular church meetings

"Encourage one another daily, as long as it is called Today, so that none of you may be hardened by sin's deceitfulness."
– Hebrews 3:23

"Let us not give up meeting together, as some are in the habit of doing."
– Hebrews 10:26

Day 10: *Unity in Christ*

Psalm 133:1-3
- What is unity and why is it so important to have it in the church?

Ephesians 4:1-3
- How do we live a worthy life?
- Explain the meaning of each virtue mentioned in verse 2.
- If we do not possess these virtues, what will happen?
- Why does it take every effort to keep unity?

Philippians 2:1-5
- What does it mean to be one in spirit and purpose?
- How can you consider others better than yourself?
- Are you looking at your own interest or do you take genuine interest in what other disciples are doing?
- What was Jesus' attitude? Is your attitude the same as his?

Matthew 5:23-24; Matthew 18:15-17
- According to Jesus, how are you to resolve conflicts and disagreements with one another?
- To whom should you go first?
- Is there anyone in the church with whom you need to go and settle a problem or dispute?

Today's Take Away

1. Think about your relationships in the body of Christ. Pray and work to be unified with all your brothers and sisters.

2. Continue memorizing and meditating on your second new value and habit.

Day 11: *Worship in Spirit and Truth*

John 4:22-24

- Does it matter where you go to worship God?
- What two things do you want to make sure you worship in?
- What do you think it means to worship in spirit and truth?
- Should you want to worship with a group that teaches an unbiblical way of being saved?
- If they aren't really saved do they have the Holy Spirit in them?
- If they don't have the Holy Spirit in them and teach an unbiblical way of being saved, then is that worshipping in spirit and in truth?

Acts 17:10-11

- When it comes to what other churches teach and practice; what should you do before you ever visit?

Today's Take Away

1. Our church is not the only church going to heaven, but make sure that before you go and visit other churches that you find out what they teach about the gospel, how to obey it in baptism, and Jesus' call to discipleship. Remember, we will be judged as individuals, not as a movement.

2. When you are traveling always look for a church where you can worship in spirit and truth

3. Continue memorizing and meditating on your second new value and habit.

Day 12: *I Will Have Family Pressures*

Mark 3:20-21
- Why do you think Jesus' family was upset with him?
- What would have happened if Jesus had agreed with them?
- Has anyone in your family ever tried to stop you from serving God because they thought you were becoming too fanatical?

John 7:1-9
- What did Jesus' own brothers think about him?
- Why can family members be the most skeptical of our conversion and faith in Christ?
- Why didn't Jesus do what his family wanted?

Matthew 10:34-39
- Why can genuine love for God bring conflict to families.
- Why does God require we love him more than even our own parents or siblings?
- List some examples of ways we can love our families more than Jesus.

Today's Take Away

1. Pray for your family and continue to show them the love of God. If need be, discuss any family pressures you are experiencing with your Discipleship partner or with a mature Christian.

2. Continue memorizing and meditating on your second new value and habit.

Day 13: *I Will Deal with Discouragement*

The prophet Elijah had just experienced some tremendous victories from God: The destruction of 450 false prophets and the first rainfall in 3 ½ years because of his earnest prayer (See 1 Kings 18:1-40 and James 5:17-18). But then he became afraid and discouraged.

1 Kings 19:1-8
- Why did Elijah feel so overwhelmed?
- What are some things that make you feel like giving up?
- How did the angel of the Lord encourage Elijah?
- What does this lesson teach you? How can you overcome discouragement?

Ecclesiastes 4:9-10
- There is a saying that says there is strength in numbers. How would the teaching of this passage benefit you when you are discouraged?

Psalm 103:2-12
- When you are discouraged, remember God's gifts. As the hymn says, "Count your many blessings. Name them one by one. Count your many blessings see what God has done."

Today's Take Away

1. When you feel discouraged, do the following:
   a. Pray. 1 Peter 5:7 says, *"Cast all your anxiety on him because he cares for you."*
   b. Counting your many blessings.
   c. Keep busy in the work of the Lord. Galatians 6:9 says, *"Let us not become weary in doing good, for at the proper time we will reap a harvest if we do not give up."*

2. Continue memorizing and meditating on your second new value and habit.

Day 14: *Trials of Many Kinds*

James 1:2-4
- List the reasons why God allows us to go through trials.
- What should your attitude be towards the trials that come your way?
- What trials do you have in your life right now?

James 1:12-15
- How can you persevere through trials and stand the test?
- Where do temptations come from?
- What things tempt you?
- Have you talked about your temptations with God? If you need prayers and encouragement, share your temptations with your discipleship partner or with a mature Christian.

Hebrews 3:12-14
- What happens when you face trials?
- How are we deceived by sin?
- What happens when your heart becomes sinful?
- What can you do to fight the deceitfulness of sin?
- How often then do you need encouragement if you want to stay faithful?

Today's Take Away

1. Talk about the trials and temptations you face with your discipleship partner or with a mature disciple. Feel free to discuss your attitude about the trials you face.

2. Have a positive mindset towards the trials you face. Put your faith in God, for he will see you through all your trials.

2. Learn to pray to the Lord in this manner, saying: "Father, do not take away my trials, rather, help me through them. May my life glorify your kingdom. Amen."

2. Continue memorizing and meditating on your second new value and habit.

Day 15: God's Word Guides My Life

We have the words and wisdom of the living God in our hands. We can either let the Creator of the Universe guide our lives or let our broken, foolish and deceived selves lead. One way leads to life and the other leads to death! Why don't you let go and let God direct your life?

Proverbs 16:25
- What happens when you follow your own ways?

Proverbs 3:3-5
- From verse 3, if you are going to let God lead your life what must you do with all of your heart?
- How do you think leaning on your own understanding will get in the way of you trusting God and his Word?

Matthew 7:24-28
- What are you like if you build your life on God's Word?
- What are you like if you build your life based on your own human understanding?
- If you want a life that will stand forever what must you put into practice (verse 24)?

Today's Take Away

1. Think about your life before becoming a disciple. What dominated your thinking?

2. What guided your actions?

3. How much did your friends influence the way you lived?

4. Pray every day God will help to make the new changes he wants for you.

5. Take an index card and write down the statement and two scriptures from the next page. Over the next several days take the index card with you everywhere you go and memorize the statement and the two scriptures.

(I) Let God's Word Guide my Life.

(Therefore, I) Biblically Memorize and Meditate.

"This is love for God: to obey His commands."
– 1 John 5:3

"Oh, how I love your law! I meditate on it all day long."
– Psalms 119:97

Day 16: *Obey God*

The mark of a true disciple is obedience to the teachings of God. Jesus said, *"If you hold to my teaching, you are really my disciples"* (John 8:31).

Matthew 7:21; Luke 6:46; John 14:15; John 15:14
- These four passages give us insight as to what it means to make Jesus Lord and friend of our lives. How is our friendship, love and service to Christ expressed?
- How is friendship towards God demonstrated?

Joshua 1:8
- What does the word meditate mean?
- Do you find yourself merely reading the word of God or do you meditate on it?

1 John 5:3
- How is real love for God demonstrated?
- If you feel that obeying God is a burden, what does that indicate about your heart and faith?
- Are you showing God how much you love him?

James 1:21-25
- How is the word of God to be accepted?
- Are we just listeners, or do we actually obey the Word?

Today's Take Away

1. Obey the word of God with all your heart and soul. Meditate on it daily. Never turn from it and never compromise. Strive to humbly and consistently obey it.

2. Continue memorizing and meditating on your third new value and habit.

Day 17: Wrestling with Doubts

1 Corinthians 15:1-4, 11-14
- Paul preached the Gospel to these Corinthians. At first, they believed what Paul taught them but later on, they started to doubt what they once believed and practiced. What were they beginning to doubt?
- Do you have doubts on doctrinal issues that you once accepted as a new disciple?
- Write down any doubts that are bothering you and discuss them with your Discipleship partner or a mature Christian.

Galatians 1:6-9; Galatians 2:4; Galatians 5:2-10
- The Galatians, like the Corinthians, believed the Gospel preached to them. However, later they started to doubt what they were taught at first. Who was responsible for creating these doubts?
- Why is important to search the scriptures and not just accept what others are telling you about God's Word?
- How did Paul help restore these Christians back to the true Gospel?
- How do we express our faith through love?

Today's Take Away

1. If you have any questions or doubts regarding doctrinal issues, discuss them with your Discipleship partner or a mature Christian who is seasoned in the word of God.

2. Continue memorizing and meditating on your third new value and habit.

Day 18: Disputable Matters

Romans 14:1-8

- What are some disputable matters among Christians today?
- Apart from the clear doctrinal truths the Bible teaches (Ephesians 4:4-6), what should your attitude be toward those who see these things differently than you?
- Looking down on someone who comes to a different conclusion than you do in regard to a "disputable matter" is called "passing judgement" on them: How do you think God looks at you when you do that?

Romans 14:16-23

- In verse 22, what does the Bible say to do when you disagree about something that doesn't relate to salvation?
- Do you keep quiet about disputable matters or do you feel you always have to voice your opinion? (see Proverbs 18:2).
- Are you doing anything that could cause others to stumble?
- What is the kingdom of God about?
- What is God teaching you in verse 19?
- Is God being glorified with the way you are living now?

Romans 15:1

- If someone is spiritually weak what should you do?
- If you think they are weak because of what they believe about a "disputable matter", do you think you are "passing judgement" on them?

Today's Take Away

1. Do you have questions about what is right and wrong for a Christian? Find out from your discipleship partner or from a mature believer whether these are disputable matters and come to your own conclusions.

2. Continue memorizing and meditating on your third new value and habit.

Day 19: *Holding On to the Truth*

2 Timothy 2:14-21
- What value is there in quarreling about words and what does it do to those who listen to it?
- Do you ever quarrel about words? If so, what must you do?
- How can you train yourself to be an "approved workman"?
- How can you avoid godless chatter?

1 Timothy 1:18-20
- How do you fight the good fight?
- How can a disciple shipwreck their faith?
- Read about Hymenaeus (2 Timothy 2:17-18) and Alexander (2 Timothy 4:14-15).
  - What happens to people who turn away from God?
  - What are some ways false brothers may harm others?

2 Timothy 4:15-16
- Have people been noticing positive and progressive changes in your Christian walk?
- Are you watching your life and doctrine? In other words, are you practicing what you preach?

2 Timothy 2:23-26
- How should you treat someone who opposes your teaching?
- What is your hope for those you gently instruct (verse 25)?

Today's Take Away

1. Discuss with your Discipleship partner any questions about doctrine or the church that you do not understand.

2. Study the word of God on a daily basis and never let go of the truth you learn from the Holy Scriptures. As Jude 1:3 says, *"contend for the faith that was once for all entrusted to the saints."*

3. Continue memorizing and meditating on your third new value and habit.

Day 20: I Will Learn from Others

Matthew 18:1-4
- What kind of heart does God want us to have?
- What qualities of children do we need to imitate?

Matthew 28:18-20
- From verse 20, what should you do with younger disciples?
- Read 1 Timothy 4:12.
  - Can a Christian be young in age, yet mature in Christ?
  - What should your attitude be when you are being taught, discipled or corrected by a mature Christian who is younger in age?

Ephesians 4:11-13
- From verse 11, from whom do other disciples learn?
- Where do we find the teachings of the apostles and prophets?
- Evangelists are preachers, pastors are elders, and teachers are those who instruct, counsel or disciple others.
- From verses 12–13, list the reason(s) why we are to learn from such persons?

Hebrews 13:7, 17
- Do you submit to those who lead and teach you?
- Do you imitate the faith of those who lead and teach you?
- Are you a pleasure to teach?

Today's Take Away

1. Seek mature disciples out and ask them questions.

2. If you are a young disciple yet older in age, do not look down on anyone because of their physical age. Rather, learn from those whom God has given insight.

3. Take an index card and write down the statement and scriptures on the next page. Over the next several days take the index card with you everywhere you go and memorize the statement and the two scriptures.

(I) Understand my need for godly training.

"Teach them to obey everything I have commanded."
– Matthew 28:20

(Therefore, I) Invite discipling in my life.

"Let us consider how we may spur one another on towards love and good deeds."
– Hebrews 10:24

Day 21: Being Open and Honest

Psalm 32:2
- What does it mean to have a deceitful spirit?
- Do you have hidden motives in your relationships in the church.

John 1:47
- What type of man was Nathaniel?
- Write down the characteristics that Nathaniel must have possessed.
- Would Jesus say the same things of you?

John 15:15
- What did Jesus share with his disciples?
- Are you this kind of a friend to other disciples?
- Do you share your life with those whom you are closest to in the church?

2 Corinthians 6:11-13
- What was Paul trying to encourage the Corinthians to do?
- What does Paul mean when he said, We have spoken freely to you and we opened wide our hearts to you?
- Are you speaking honestly and opening your heart to others, especially in your discipleship group?

Today's Take Away

1. Spend some time today writing down some feelings, plans, or struggles that you haven't been sharing with others. Discuss these things with those in your discipleship group or with a mature Christian whom you are close to.

2. Continue memorizing and meditating on your fourth new value and habit.

Day 22: Confessing Sin

Psalm 32:1-7
- How did the Psalmist feel when he was hiding his sin and not confessing them to God?
- When he got open and confessed them, what happened?
- Are there sins you have been afraid to confess? If so, why not follow the example of the Psalmist? (See 1 John 1:9).

Proverbs 28:13; James 5:16
- Can we conceal our sins from God?
- What effect will concealed sin have in our life?
- Who do we need to confess our sins to besides God?

Psalm 66:18-19
- The word "cherish" according to Webster's means to "hold dear, feel or show affection for." A second definition is to "entertain or harbor in the mind deeply and resolutely." What happens if we conceal or cherish sin?

Luke 8:17; 1 Corinthians 4:5
- Why is it foolish to try to keep sins hidden?

Today's Take Away

1. Take some time to think about any sins—whether attitudes, action, or thoughts—that are troubling you and confess them to God and renounce them today.

2. Please confess these sins to either your discipleship partner or to another mature Christian and pray with that disciple. For our brother, James, in James 5:16 encourages us to confess our sins to one another and to pray for one another that we may be healed. The prayers of righteous men are powerful and effective. Amen!

3. Continue memorizing and meditating on your fourth new value and habit.

Day 23: *I'll Take Correction*

Galatians 2:11-16

- What was Peter's sin?
- How did his bad example affect others?
- Why did Paul correct him publicly and not privately? (See Timothy 5:20 and Matthew 18:15).

2 Corinthians 7:8-13

- How did the Corinthians respond to Paul's correction?
- What is the difference between worldly and godly sorrow?
- How does God want you to respond to correction?
- Has anyone corrected you lately?
- If so, how did you respond?
- Were they encouraged by your response?

Proverbs 15:31-32

- What does correction bring?

Proverbs 10:17

- Those who receive correction have the potential to what?
- Those who hate correction have the potential to what?

Proverbs 27:6

- Who are your true friends?
- What will an enemy do?

Today's Take Away

1. Correction is designed to help your walk with Jesus. Do not allow yourself to feel unloved when you are corrected. It's not to your benefit. When you are being corrected, you are actually being loved and cared for.

2. Continue memorizing and meditating on your fourth new value and habit.

Day 24: *I Will Pursue Holiness*

1 Peter 1:13-23
- Now that you are a child of God, what are you called to be?
- Why does God call you to be this way?
- From verse 14, to what does Peter contrast holiness?
- How does obeying God purify our hearts?

1 Peter 4:1-5
- Define each item listed in verse 3.
- How will people in the world react to a holy life?
- To whom shall we give an account for the way we lived?

Acts 19:18-19
- From verse 19, how did these new disciples express their desire to be holy?
- Do you have any books, CDs, videos, clothing or any other paraphernalia that is offensive to God that needs to be thrown away? If so, get rid of them now and pray to God, thanking him for salvation and freedom from sin.

Psalm 119:9-16
- How can you keep your way pure?
- From verse 11, what encouragement does God's Word offer you and why?
- Do you—on a daily basis—study and meditate on the word of God?

Today's Take Away

1. Ask your Discipleship partner—or mature Christian—who know you well—if they see any worldly attitudes or habits in your life that you need to change.

2. Be receptive towards their critiques and thank them for their desire to help you become more like Jesus.

3. Continue memorizing and meditating on your fourth new value and habit.

Day 25: Walking As Jesus Did

1 John 2:5-6

- Think back over the past several days since you started this series. Are you walking like Jesus?

Mark 1:21-28

- What was different about the way Jesus taught?
- Why did Jesus teach both privately and publicly?

Mark 1:29-34

- How late do you think Jesus worked that night?
- Do you think he felt tired?
- Why did he work so hard?
- Why did healing (meeting the needs of people) and teaching God's Word always go hand-in-hand in the ministry of Jesus.

Mark 1:35-39

- Jesus got up very early the next day. Why?

Mark 2:13-17

- What kinds of people did Jesus make friends with and why?
- How do you interact with "sinners"? Would they consider you a friend?
- Are you making new friends to share the gospel with?

Today's Take Away

1. Write down the things you've learned from today's study and apply them to your life today.

2. Continue memorizing and meditating on your fourth new value and habit.

Day 26: I Will Go and Make Disciples

Mark 16:15; Matthew 28:19-20
- From Matthew 28:19, what are you called to go make?
- From Mark 16:15, what does disciple-making start with?
- From verse 16, how does one respond to the gospel?
- From Matthew, after their baptism what's your responsibility?

2 Timothy 2:1-7
- How are you to follow the example of a soldier, an athlete and a farmer? Be specific.
- Are you reliable in terms of keeping appointments, being punctual, and taking direction?
- Would Timothy have chosen you to teach others? Why?

1 Corinthians 9:19-27
- How is being a disciple-maker like running a race?
- What happens if an athlete does not train or beat his or her body?
- What happens if you do not train and discipline yourself as a disciple?

Today's Take Away

1. Ask the Lord to stir within you a deep, burning love for the lost. Ask him to enable you to speak the gospel effectively and boldly. Ask God to use you to bring others to him.

2. List ways you can be more disciplined in the area of discipleship, especially in the area of evangelism. Share it with your Discipleship partner or with a mature, evangelistic Christian.

3. Take an index card and write down the statement and scriptures on the next page. Over the next several days take the index card with you everywhere you go and memorize the statement and the two scriptures.

(I) Enjoy bringing souls to Christ.

"God our Savior who wants all men to be saved."

– 1 Timothy 2:3-4

(Therefore, I) Tell others the Good News.

"Go into all the world and preach the good news to all creation."

– Mark 16:15

V.A.L.U.E.S. & H.A.B.I.T.S. *of spiritual growth*

Day 27: *Too Good to Keep*

2 Kings 7:3-11
- These four lepers were starving and had no hope. Before you were baptized, how were you like these four lepers?
- How is the kingdom of God like an unlimited feast?
- In verse 9, these men thought it wrong to withhold this good news to themselves. Do you tend to keep the good news of salvation to yourself? (see Mark 16:15).

Romans 10:1-4, 14-21
- Do you feel like Paul does about the lost?
- Who does God send to preach?
- Why is it essential to share the good news of Jesus?
- Will everyone accept the good news? If not, why not?
- Why is it important to preach no matter what the response?

Acts 4:23-29
- These disciples prayed to God for boldness in sharing the message of salvation. Do you ask God to enable you to speak with boldness the good news of Christ to others?

Today's Take Away

1. Share your faith with your family, friends and coworkers. Be determined to not allow yourself to be discouraged by people's poor reaction to the Gospel.

2. Pray to the Father for boldness and effectiveness in sharing your faith.

3. If you are new to public evangelism, ask your discipleship partner or a mature disciple to go evangelizing with you.

4. If you get a person who is interested in learning more about the Bible, get their phone number and set up a study time with them. Take a mature Christian with you to the study.

5. Continue memorizing and meditating on your fifth new value and habit.

Day 28: *I Am Saved to Save*

Mark 16:15; 1 Corinthians 15:1-4; 1 Peter 2:9-10
- God calls all his disciples to share the gospel of Jesus Christ:
- What does it mean to be a royal priesthood?
- What message are you called to declare?
- Are you declaring God's praises with the lost, or just handing out an invitation?

2 Corinthians 5:14-21
- How can you tell if you're living for yourself, or for God?
- Go to the dictionary and look up the word ambassador.
- What does it mean to be Christ's ambassador?
- What does *make an appeal* and *implore* mean?
- What attitude should you have toward the lost?

Acts 17:16-34
- Why was Paul distressed after touring Athens?
- What are some sights around your city that distress you?
- Why did Paul begin his message by commending the Athenians for being very religious?

1 Corinthians 9:19-27
- How did Paul use his freedom in Christ?
- How are you using your freedom?
- Are you using your freedom to impact others for God?

Today's Take Away

1. Write at least four things you have learned today about evangelism from this study.

2. Make a spiritual contact list of those whom you are in contact with. Pray to God to use you to help them come to know Him. Try to set up a Bible study with those on your spiritual contact list.

3. Continue memorizing and meditating on your fifth new value and habit.

Day 29: I Have the Hope of New Creation

Revelation 20:11-15
- Take time to imagine what "Judgment Day" will be like!
- Who will be present on the final "Judgment Day"?
- What emotions will be present?

Revelation 21:1-8
- Who is the bride of Christ?
- Describe the new creation.
- What sins are listed that will result in the second death?
- Who will suffer the second death?

Revelation 22:1-6
- What other eternal joys will be in heaven?
- Why does God want us to know these words are trustworthy and true?

Revelation 22:14-15
- Why are you such a blessed person?
- What might it mean when it says in verse 14, *"Blessed are those who have washed their robes."?*
- Who will be shut out from the presence of God?

Today's Take Away

1. Pray about what God promises in eternal life and be thankful for your salvation.

2. When you're asked, "How are you?", one good response is: *I am blessed!*

3. Continue memorizing and meditating on your fifth new value and habit.

Day 30: Shining Like Stars

Philippians 2:14-16

- How does a disciple hold out the word of life to others?
- What kind of example do you need to be to those around you?
- Have you had a complaining or argumentative spirit in your Christian walk?
- What circumstances usually bring out your complaints, or argumentative spirit?

1 Corinthians 9:19-23

- What does Paul mean when he says, *"To the weak, I became weak, to win the weak"*?
- How can you be a slave to everyone? Give some practical examples.
- What are some of the blessings of sharing the gospel?

Matthew 5:13-16

- What is the purpose of salt?
- What is the purpose of light?
- What did Jesus mean when he said you are the salt of the earth and the light of the world?
- Why does the world need to see our good deeds?

Today's Take Away

1. Ask the Lord to use your life to impact those around you for his glory.

2. Look for ways to be the salt in every conversation and circumstance.

3. Continue memorizing and meditating on your fifth new value and habit.

2 Timothy 2:1-2
- Paul the apostle commanded Timothy, the young preacher, to share with others the gospel that had been given to him.
- Thus we learn the gospel and the Christian way of life so we can pass it on to future generations.

Matthew 10:32-33
- Jesus wants you to speak his name and show his way of life to those you know and meet while living your life.
- You cannot be ashamed of God, or the principles and way of a godly life he wants you to live before others.
- You need to be aware that Satan will do all he can to keep you from being what Jesus wants in your life.

1 Corinthians 15:1-4
- You obeyed the gospel (Death, Burial, and Resurrection of Jesus).
- You have knowledge God wants you to share with others.

Mark 16:15-16
- Jesus gave you this responsibility.
- When you realize how much God loves you and saved you though Jesus' blood, you will want to share that good news with others.

Today's Take Away

1. Pray to God for courage to speak the name of Jesus to your friends and loved ones.
2. Examine the study guide and gospel presentation that was used with you when you became a Christian.
3. Pray to God to open your eyes to see the opportunities he is giving you at this moment.
4. Continue memorizing and meditating on your fifth new value and habit.

Day 32: *I Am Saved to Serve*

Matthew 25:31-46
- When we serve those who are hurting in the kingdom, who are we really serving?
- Which of the six things listed in verses 35-36 have you done recently?

Ephesians 2:10
- What has God created us for?
- Make a list of some good works that you could do.

1 Peter 4:8-11
- What does loving each other do for us?
- Have you been offering hospitality to other disciples?
- Why should we never grumble when serving others?
- How can you improve in this and do more?
- Why do you think God wants you to be giving to others?

Galatians 6:9-10
- Who does God want us to help?
- Who in your discipleship group (or in the church) has special needs right now that you could help?

Today's Take Away

1. Who can you help today? Why not help them now?

2. Make plans with other Christians to help those who are in need this week. If you don't know how you can help, seek advice from your discipleship partner or a mature Christian. Always keep this in mind—we are family; we need each other!

3. Take an index card and write down the statement and scriptures on the next page. Over the next several days take the index card with you everywhere you go and memorize the statement and the two scriptures.

(I) Sincerely care about the needs of others. **(Therefore, I) Serve others with my S.H.A.P.E.**

"Each of you should look not only to your own interests, but also to the interests of others."
– Philippians 2:4

"Each one should use whatever gift he has received to serve others."
– 1 Peter 4:10

The Bible says that you are a *"workmanship"* literary a "master piece" of God's *(Ephesians 2:10).* Later in that same verse the Bible goes on to say that God uniquely made **you** for a specific purpose. What is that? *"For works of service that God prepared in advance for you to do."* In other words, your purpose in life is to discover your unique SHAPE so that you can serve God with it.

Discovering your SHAPE is not only critical to your service to God, but it's also critical for your relationships in the church. Knowing your SHAPE can give you a common language to use to better understand yourself and others in Christ. Knowing my own SHAPE has given me so much more clarity and confidence that God has a unique purpose for my life. Also, I have seen other relationships improve by having a common language to better understand and value their differences. So, let's spend the next few days discovering your unique SHAPE. What does SHAPE stand for?

S-piritual Gifts, H-eart, A-bilities, P-ersonality, E-xperiences

SPIRITUAL GIFTS

Here's what the Bible says about spiritual gifts. *"A spiritual gift is given to each of us as a means of helping the entire church"* (1 Corinthians 12:4-7 msg). Spiritual gifts are given to Christians for the specific purpose of building up the church. And the church doesn't just mean your local congregation, but the worldwide kingdom of God. In other words, you have gifts that God wants to use!

We don't have all the same spiritual gifts. *"God has arranged the parts in the body, every one of them, just as he wanted them to be. If they were all one part, where would the body be? As it is, there are many parts, but one body"* (1 Corinthians 12:18-19). As each one of us does our part we build up the church in love (Ephesians 4:16).

HEART

Your heart represents what you are passionate about. What do you love? What topics make you excited? Psalm 37 says, *"Delight in the Lord and he will give you your heart's desires."* Some Christians feel like they have to give up of their heart's desires when they come to Christ. It's the exact opposite. We work the hardest when we are passionate about something. God made us this way. Take your passions and put it into serving other for God's glory!

ABILITIES

Abilities are different from spiritual gifts in that spiritual gifts are a very specific list found in the Bible that are for building up the church. On the other hand abilities are any and everything else you are good at that God can use to love and serve others.

In the Old Testament, Exodus 31, *"The Lord said to Moses, look I have chosen Bezalel son of Uru, grandson of Hur from the tribe of Judah. I have filled him with the Spirit of God, given him wisdom, intelligence and skill in all kinds of crafts."* God has given you some incredible abilities. Some of you are unbelievably talented. But a talent without passion or without a spiritual gift is just used for yourself which becomes empty.

PERSONALITY

Your personality greatly affects how you use your spiritual gifts, heart, and abilities. Maybe you're an extrovert, or an introvert. Neither is better than the other. But many of us would be so much more effective in our ministry if we were more aware of our personality type and those around us.

EXPERIENCES

God wants to use both your good and bad life experiences to make a major difference in the world. There are so many people out there hurting who think that they are all alone in their pain. By sharing with others the pain, trials, and tribulations that God has brought you out of you can also share the comfort that God has brought you. For many this is the first step of healing.

Also, understanding your past experiences will also help you understand why you have the desires you have, your personality and where your personal habits come from.

Over the next several days you will discover your S.H.A.P.E., and I pray that you will use it to serve others and enrich your relationships in Christ. You are needed in the body of Christ and there is a special place for you to use your unique gifts.

Your **S.H.A.P.E.** Chart

S _____

H _____

_____

A _____

P _____

E _____

Day 34: Discover Your Spiritual Gifts

The following are a list of statements that describe someone with a specific spiritual gift found in scripture. To discover the unique gifts that God has given you complete the following steps.

Step One: As you read each statement write the number 3 next to the statement if it strongy describes you, 2 if it generally describes you, 1 if it rarely describes you and 0 if it doesn't describe you at all. Don't number your survey based on what you want to be tomorrow, but rather who you are today. If you have any difficulty answering a question feel free to ask someone close to you who can give you an objective opinion.

Step Two: When you are finished numbering all of the statements tally the total for each spiritual gift and write the individual totals next to each gift.

Step Three: Find your top 3-4 spiritual gifts and write them next to "Spiritual Gifts" on your S.H.A.P.E. chart.

Administration: (1 Cor. 12:28) Coordination of people and projects
- I seek to make projects more efficient (i.e. by organizing processes).
- I enjoy delegating tasks to the right people for a ministry or project.
- People look to me to keep a project well-organized and run smoothly.
- In a project environment, I make sure that no detail is overlooked.
- People rely on me to file, research, schedule tasks and appointments.

Discernment: (1 Cor. 12:10) Distinguish what's from God or Satan
- I have a sense of when someone is speaking/acting for God or Satan.
- I am alert to when people are under spiritual attack or being blessed.
- I am alert to when people are seeking things for themselves or God.
- I am a good judge of struggles, character and people's likes/dislikes.
- I notice things others miss and am aware of opportunities and danger.

Encouragement: (Romans 12:8) Build up others through word or deed
- By word or deed, I help others to overcome their fears and realize their potential.
- I positively affirm people's abilities and accomplishments.
- I enjoy seeing and communicating the good that I see in others.
- When people are discouraged I try to "lift their spirits."
- I write notes or speak to people to help them through difficult times.

Evangelist: (Ephesians 4:11) Lead church/mission teams to reach the lost
- I am passionate about sharing the gospel with others.
- I am able to mobilize others to reach out to unreached communities.
- I am able to understand and interact in different cultural settings.
- I am able to be in a non-Christian setting and easily interact.
- I memorize scripture so I am ready to teach and defend the gospel.

Faith: (1 Cor. 12:9) Unwavering confidence in God's power and plan
- I have unwavering trust that God will guard, protect, and provide.
- When others doubt, I believe firmly that God's will will be done.
- I don't let obstacles shake my belief that God will always triumph.
- No matter what the challenge, I know that God will overcome.
- Knowing God will overcome allows me to always remain claim.

Giving: (Romans 12:8) Being generous with your personal resources
- My financial state does not hinder me in giving generously to others.
- When I see or hear about needy people, I sacrifice so that I can help.
- When I receive funds I think of how I can share it with the needy.
- I live by the mantre that "it is more blessed to give than receive."
- I actively seek out people or ministries that need financial assistance.

Helping: (1 Cor. 12:28) Support or assist someone else's project
- When someone has too much to do, I enjoy lightening their load.
- I don't enjoy leading projects, but rather helping, however is needed.
- When I see others working on something, I ask, "How can I help?"
- I seek to find ways that I can assist a person to make their job easier.
- I am content to provide assistance to those in charge of a task.

Hospitality: (1 Peter 4:9) Warmly welcome and connect others
- I enjoy hosting events, parties, and meals that bring people together.
- I love meeting new people and making them feel welcome.
- If someone needs a place to stay, I want to open up my home.
- I am not afraid to welcome strangers, or new people into my home.
- I go out of my way to make sure that people do not feel "left out."

Knowledge: (1 Cor. 12:8) Insatiable hunger to learn about the Bible
- I have an intense hunger to grow in biblical knowledge.
- I am able to learn and understand deep spiritual truths.
- I am able to memorize and connect many biblical passages/truths.
- I have a deep understanding of God and his will.
- People look to me to provide insight into deeper spiritual truths.

Leadership: (Romans 12:8) Direct people and resouces towards a goal
- I take initiative in beginning a new ministry or charting a new course.
- Others seem to naturally look to me for direction and guidance.
- I am able to share a vision that motivates others to go a certain way.
- I am not afraid to take responsibility for major ministries, or projects.
- People seem to naturally trust my ability, skill level, and judgment.

Mercy: (Romans 12:8) Sensitivity towards those hurting or struggling
- When others are too harsh on people's mistakes, I protect them.
- I desire to comfort and reassure those who experience hardship.
- I have compassion for those who struggle in their Christian walk.
- When people sin or stumble, I am there to help them recover.
- I show kindness to others even when it seems they don't deserve it.

Pastor/Elder: (Ephesians 4:11) Care for and oversee God's local church
- I believe I meet the qualifications of an Elder in 1 Timothy 3.
- I enjoy helping people grow in their Christian walk and maturity.
- I enjoy ministering to young, weak, or struggling Christians.
- I find that people seek me out to talk about problems in their lives.
- People follow me because they know that I love and care for them.

Service: (Romans 12:7) Complete unfinished tasks in God's work
- I take pleasure in doing the unnoticed "behind the scenes" work.
- I volunteer to help in whatever tasks needs to be done.
- I like to "use my hands" in serving.
- I don't hunger for recognition when serving others.
- I enjoy doing things that others often consider "menial" or "tedious."
- However I can serve, I am ready to do any job that needs to be done.

Teaching: (Romans 12:7) Instruct in a way others can understand
- I am able to explain the Bible in a way that others can understand.
- People seem to be engaged and respond when I teach them scripture.
- I enjoy learning scripture and sharing what I learn with others.
- People say they understand scripture much better after I explain it.
- I am good at leading Bible discussions and stimulating thought.

Wisdom: (1 Corinthians 12:8) Make scripture relevant to everyday life
- People ask for my advice when they face difficult life choices.
- I am able to help others choose the best out of multiple paths.
- When dealing with problems, I keep perspective in the big picture.
- My life experience enables me to provide practical advice to others.
- I show wisdom by providing an example for others to imitate.

Your actions reveals what you are passionate about. What do you love? What topics make you excited? What conversations make you so excited you start raising your voice? Maybe your passion is art and being creative? Maybe it's working with numbers, people, children, the poor, the elderly, etc? Maybe you just love building, creating plans, organizing, performing, writing, singing, etc.? God has given you a unique heart filled with unique passions.

Psalm 37 says, *"Delight in the Lord and he will give you your heart's desires."* Some Christians feel like they have to give up of their heart's desires when they come to Christ. It's the exact opposite. God wants you to use the desires of your heart to make a big deal out of him.

Keep in mind that there is sometimes a major discrepancy between what you are the most passionate about and what you are the most gifted with. For example, your passion could be singing, but you may not have the ability to carry a tune. If so, it's fun to keep the shower walls shaking! The point is that true fulfillment is found in the balance of who you are and who you want to be.

Maybe, you haven't been using your passions with the right motives. It's been hey look at me. I want to pursue this so that others will know I really am somebody. Let your self-ambition go and turn your passions over to God to use. Our world needs to see followers of Christ that are passionate about life and Jesus. Take your passions and put it on display so that the world can see what a passionate life in Christ looks like.

As time goes on your passions will probably change and mature. This is part of our life's journey. For many of us we need to try new things and overcome certain fears in order to discover what we are really passionate about.

Write down the top 1-4 things you are passionate about on your S.H.A.P.E. chart next to **Heart.**

What's your Love Language?

As you were growing up you learned a language at home. This is called your primary or first language. Some people learn more than one but for most people, even if we learn a second language later on in life we will always be more comfortable when communicating in our "native" tongue, or our primary language.

When you come across someone who doesn't speak your language your ability to communicate is limited to hand gestures, facial expressions, or acting out ideas. You can still communicate but it's difficult—there's a lot of room for misunderstanding. To communicate effectively with someone who doesn't know your language you have to become proficient at theirs.

In the area of love it's the same. According to Dr. Gary Chapman we all have a unique love language that when "spoken" makes us feel loved. In Chapman's theory, there are five primary ways in which people express and understand love. These five love "languages" are:

1. **Acts of Service** (Galatians 5:13).
   Helping someone in the areas of life that are the most important to them (not necessarily to you).

2. **Words of Affirmation** (Ephesians 4:29).
   Giving someone verbal appreciation, compliments and general encouragement.

3. **Gifts** (2 Corinthians 8:7).
   A visible symbol of your love that communicates, "when you weren't around, I was thinking of you."

4. **Quality Time** (Acts 2:42).
   Giving someone your undivided attention. Having quality conversation. Doing activities together, etc.

5. **Physical Touch** (Mark 1:41-42).
   Warm hugs, holy kisses, pats on the back, light touches, etc.

Chapman believes that while some people can often express and understand love in any number of these languages, we all have a primary love language (or two) through which we are most comfortable expressing and receiving love. Often times in life our greatest frustration in our relationships comes from not understanding our own love language or the person we are trying to communicate our love to. For example, if my love language is gifts, but someone does acts of service for me, I won't feel as loved.

Write down your top 1-2 love languages on your S.H.A.P.E. chart next to **Heart**.

Day 36: Discover Your Abilities

After talking about your Spiritual gifts and heart, today we turn to your Abilities. There is a distinct difference between your spiritual gifts and your abilities. Spiritual gifts are a very specific list found in the Bible that are designed to build up the church. Abilities are any and everything else that you are good at.

Some abilities are natural, other abilities are learned. Some things you were just born to do well. Other things you've developed the skills for over a period of time. Both are abilities.

In the Old Testament, Exodus 31, *"The Lord said to Moses, look I have chosen Bezalel son of Uru, grandson of Hur from the tribe of Judah. I have filled him with the Spirit of God, given him wisdom, intelligence and skill in all kinds of crafts."* God has given you some incredible abilities. Some of you are unbelievably talented.

Nothing about you is a mistake, or was left to chance. You are one of God's masterpieces (Ephesians 2:10). But you need to remember, your abilities need to be used to bring God glory and serve others. 1 Corinthians 10:31 says, *"So whether you eat or dink, or whatever you do, do it all for the glory of God."* Whatever you do, whatever you have the ability to do, God wants you use that for his glory.

The Bible is full of people who had abilities they used for God's glory. Art, building, baking, embroidering, fishing, music, painting, carpentry, tent making, etc. Church history is full of the same kind of people. Luke was a doctor. Paul was a tent maker. Peter was a fisherman. Jesus was a carpenter. All of them (and many others) used their god-given abilities for the good of God's Kingdom. God has a place in the church for every ability and every talent to be used, and to make a difference in the world.

As an individual disciple, you have a unique set of talents and abilities. They're yours and you're the only one who can use them. Because they're part of your SHAPE. God has given these abilities to you so that you can accomplish your service to the kingdom of God. Hebrews says that God will *"equip you with everything good for doing his will"* (Hebrews 13:21).

If God equips you then God also expects you to use what you've been given. If you have a talent or ability for music, then God expects that you will find a way to serve using that ability. If you can't carry a tune, God doesn't expect you to lead the choir.

The abilities you have are a strong indication of what God wants you to do with your life (and what God doesn't want you to do). Abilites aren't given to you to just make a living, or to amuse you in your down-time. They are given to you to SHAPE your ministry.

Although I want you to come up with your own list of abilities and then write down your top 1-4 abilities on your S.H.A.P.E. chart next to **Abilities**, here is one exercise to help you get started.

Life is like a road trip with a group of friends, and it takes four major abilities to make the trip successful.

Destination: Some people are destination oriented. They ask, "Where are we going?" They are dreamers, visionaries and motivators. But the destination means nothing with out directions.

Directions: Some people are direction oriented. They ask, "How will we get there step-by-step?" They are planners, strategic thinkers, and information gatherers. But directions means nothing without a driver to get you there.

Driver: Some people are driver oriented. They say, "Let's go!" They are doers, executers, they can't sit still. But a Driver means nothing if he gets there alone without any Driving Partners.

Driving Partner: Some people are driving partner oriented. They say, "I don't care where we go as long as we go together." They are relationships builders.

Of these for D's which of these is the most important one? **None!** It's only a successful road trip when all four do their part. The truth is we all have at least a little of all 4, but there are usually 1 or 2 that we are the strongest in. Which are you the strongest in? Write your top 1-2 D's on your S.H.A.P.E. chart next to **Abilities**, and then finish by adding whatever addition abilities God has given you. If you aren't sure what your abilities are ask someone close to you what they think you're dominant gifts are.

Day 37: *Discover Your Personality*

In each box chose the words that best describe your personality. Double the number of words you chose and record that number. Write in your answer on your S.H.A.P.E. chart 1-4 highest to lowest.

Lion/Paul type: "Let's do it now!"

Likes authority	Confident	Firm
Enjoys challenges	Problem solver	Bold
Goal driven	Strong willed	Self reliant
Persistent	Takes charge	Determined
Enterprising	Competitive	Productive
Purposeful	Adventurous	Independent
Controlling	Action oriented	Double #:_____

Beaver/Luke type: "How was it done in the past?"

Enjoys instructions	Consistent	Reserved
Practical	Factual	Perfectionistic
Detailed	Inquisitive	Persistent
Sensitive	Accurate	Controlled
Predictable	Orderly	Conscientious
Discerning	Analytical	Precise
Scheduled	Deliberate	Double #:_____

Otter/Peter type: "Trust me. It'll work out."

Enthusiastic	Visionary	Energetic
Promoter	Mixes easily	Fun-loving
Spontaneous	Creative	Optimistic
Infectious laughter	Risk Taker	Motivator
Very verbal	Friendly	Enjoys popularity
Likes variety	Enjoys change	Group-oriented
Initiator	Inspirational	Double #:_____

Golden Retriever/John type: "Let's keep things the way they are."

Sensitive feelings	Calm	Non-demanding
Avoids conflicts	Enjoys routine	Warm and relational
Adaptable	Thoughtful	Patient
Good listener	Loyal	Even keeled
Gives in	Indecisive	Dislikes change
Dry humor	Sympathetic	Nurturing
Tolerant	Peace maker	Double #:_____

Here is a description of the four personality types:

LION/ PAUL type: This personality likes to lead. They're good at making decisions and are action-oriented. They enjoy challenges, difficult assignments, and opportunities for advancement. Because they are thinking of the goal, they can step on people to reach it. They must learn not to be bossy or to take charge in other's affairs.

> **Biblical Example:** Paul (Acts 9:3-19, John 2:12-17)
> **Strength:** Goal-oriented, strong, direct
> **Weakness:** Argumentative, forceful, hard time expressing grace

OTTER/ PETER type: This personality is very social and loves people. They enjoy being popular and influencing and motivating others. They can sometimes be hurt when people do not like them. This personality type usually have lots of friends, but not deep relationships. They like to hurry and finish jobs and they are often not done thoroughly.

> **Biblical Example:** Peter (John 21:1-22)
> **Strength:** People person, open, positive
> **Weakness:** Talks too much, permissive, doesn't follow through

GOLDEN RETRIEVER/ JOHN type: Good at making friends. Very loyal. Retriever personalities do not like big changes. They look for security. Can be very sensitive. Very caring. Has deep relationships, but usually only a couple of close friends. Wants to be loved by everyone. Looks for appreciation. Works best in a limited situation with a steady work pattern.

> **Biblical Example:** Abraham (Genesis 12-22, John 11:33-36)
> **Strength:** Accommodating, calm, affirming
> **Weakness:** Indecisive, indifferent, too easy on other people

BEAVER/ LUKE type: Organized. This personality type often think that there is a right way to do everything and they want to do it exact that way. Beaver personalities are very creative. They desire to solve everything and they want to take their time and do it right. Beavers do not like sudden changes. They need reassurance.

> **Biblical Example:** Luke (Luke 1:1-4)
> **Strength:** High standards, order, respect
> **Weakness:** Unrealistic expectations, inflexible, perfectionist

---

Possess these qualities in increasing measure...and you will never fall!

Day 38: Discover Your Experiences

We all need to stand before God and say, "God, all that I am and all that I've been through, is yours to use to make a difference in this world." God wants to use both your good and bad life experiences.

What about the painful ones? Maybe you're thinking, "I was abused. How is God going to use that?"; "I was sexually molested. How is God going to use that?" 2 Corinthians 1:4-5 says that God *"comforts us in all our troubles, so that we can comfort those in any trouble with the comfort we ourselves have received from God. For just as the sufferings of Christ flow over into our lives, so also through Christ our comfort overflows."*

There are so many people out there hurting who think that they alone in their pain. By sharing with others the pain, trials and tribulations that God has brought you out of you, can enable you to share the comfort that God has brought you. Many people start the healing process when they realize that they are not alone. God doesn't want to waste your experiences. Even the painful ones!

Some people blame their bad experiences on God. They believe that it was God who hurt them. But God doesn't hurt us. Rather it's the consequences of free will that bring pain. Unfortunately, others are able to make choices that can deeply hurt us. In a free-choice world, bad things do happen to good people. But, don't blame God. Rather, go to God for healing and then use your experience as a testimony to help and encourage others. Just look at Paul's mindset in 1 Timothy 1:13-16. He knew his bad past, but he was going to use it as an example for others to have hope.

The first step to using your past and transforming your future is becoming aware. How can you use or change something you are not even aware of? So, do you know the experiences that have shaped who you are today? Let's spend some time today looking at three major ways your past conditions who you are today.

Verbal programming: What did you hear when you were young? Did you ever hear phrases like money is the root of all evil, don't trust anyone, don't back down from anyone, everyone's out for number one, get a good education, God wants you to be happy, you're so pretty, you need to lose weight, etc? All of these statements you heard about God, money, relationships, your body and your personality when you were young remain in your subconscious mind as part of the blueprint that is running your life. Are there any major statements that stick out to you that have shaped who you are today? For example, I know that a large part of my confidence in life comes from how encouraging and supportive my mother was. Therefore, I also understand that if I had a negative parent, that I might be a totally different person than I am today.

Modeling: What did you see when you were young? What were your parents or guardians like in the arena of their marriage, money, or their faith? Were they spenders or savers? Did you see them reading their Bible and praying, or did they have a different value system? Did they encourage you to talk to them, or to be quiet and don't talk back? Were they affectionate towards each other and towards you? Why is this so important? Like the saying goes, "We become what we see."

The Bible says, *"Bad company corrupts good character"* (1 Corinthians 15:33), and the reverse is also true.

As kids we learn just about everything from imitation. If you're not just like one of your parents or guardians then you're probably the exact opposite. Why? Ever hear of rebellion? Many of us spend our lives trying to "prove" that we are nothing like our parents.

What are the major areas of modeling that have affected you the most in life? What critical things did you see growing up that are a large part of who you are today? For example, I'm incredibly affectionate because my entire family hugged and kissed each other all of the time. This is why one of my love languages is physical touch.

Specific Incidents: What did you experience when you were young? Was your family small or large? Were you always trying to get your parents attention over your siblings? Did you have bad experiences that taught you to not trust men or women or rich/poor people, or religious people? Maybe you were physically, emotionally or sexually abused when you were younger? Unfortunately, one very bad experience can often cancel out a hundred good experiences.

Think about all of your most memorable past experiences and try to pick the top 1-4 experiences that have most influenced who you are today. You can always go back and change them later as you discover events that were more impactful than you ever imagined. You can also use this same exercise to go much deeper in your past and discover what has made you the man or woman you are today.

Write down your top 3-4 experiences in descending order on your S.H.A.P.E. chart next to **Experiences.**

Day 39: *You are Needed in the Kingdom*

Jesus said in Matthew 22:39, *"Love your neighbor as yourself."* As yourself? We all understand the "command" to love God and to love others, but we tend to overlook the fact that loving yourself is a "command" as well. Are you obeying God's command to love yourself? Or, are you constantly focused on your faults and weaknesses? When you make mistakes are you extremely critical of yourself? Do you constantly have negative statements replaying in your mind like, "You're not what you're supposed to be. You don't measure up. You've blown it too many times."

I know it is difficult for some people to believe, but God wants us to feel good about ourselves (not our sin). He wants us to be secure and to have healthy self-images. He wants us to look in the mirror and be filled with joy in who he's made us. *"The fruits of the Spirit are love, joy..."* (Galatians 5:22). This doesn't mean we are to be pride filled, but like Paul says in Romans 12:3, the first step to liking yourself is to start *"thinking of yourself with sober judgement."* We all need to take a long look in the mirror and say with sober judgement, *"By the grace of God I am what I am"* (1 Corinthians 15:10). Over the past seven days this is exactly what we've been doing.

Stop comparing yourself to others.

This was actually one of the biggest lessons I had to learn in my own life. It was my junior year at Stony Brook University and I was the student campus ministry leader at the time. My roommate was a brother in Christ and he frequently told me how convicted he was by everything I was doing on campus. He would also constantly compare how hard school was for him, and how easy school seemed to be for me. How simple he was and how great I was. At the time I really enjoyed all the ego strokes. That was until I really started to study out *Matthew 25* and the parable of the talents.

In the parable of the talents there were two key observations I discovered:

First, God gave you your talents. Whether you have, or think you have, 1, 2, 5 or 10 talents, you have done absolutely nothing to deserve them. For example, you're either born with a great singing voice or not. You can learn how to control it, or do fancy things with it, but you can't go to the store and buy a better tonal quality.

In the same way, leadership is one of my spiritual gifts (Romans 12:8). I didn't earn it. It's not a better gift than giving or serving. It was a gift from God. There were certain life experiences I've had that have developed the leadership skills in me. I didn't just look at a list and decide, "Oh, I think I'm going to become a leader."

The first thing the parable of the talents taught me was that it's totally by God's grace that I am what I am, and so stop comparing your self to others!

Second, God judges *your* faithfulness to *your* talents. God doesn't judge the one with two talents the same way he does the one with 10 talents. He judges you by what *you* do verses what *you* could do. One more time. God judges what *you* do verses what *you* could do. Not verses what John or Sarah could do, but what you could do.

After studying out Jesus' teaching in Matthew 25, we had a fellowship time, and in tears I praised my roommate because I realized that his life put mine to shame. Maybe he was a two talent person, but he was proving faithful with four. That's 100% beyond himself. He worked so hard to be his absolute best. Maybe I had more talents, but I was just coasting in life. I didn't work anywhere near as hard as he did in proving faithful with talents given to me by God.

My roommate was right when he said he spent all weekend studying just to get a B. But what I was overlooking was the fact that when he had two hours free he spent it having a quiet time with God and studying the Bible with other students. Maybe it was true that I spent less time studying to do well, but what did I do with my extra free time? Honestly, I did spend a lot of it on God, but I also spent a lot of it on selfish pursuits. But did God give me that talent so I could spend even more time on myself or more time on him? **On him!**

My roommate was comparing what he did verses what I did and he was impressed. Meanwhile, God was judging me by what I did verses what I could've done, and He wasn't impressed. Like Luke 12:48 says, *"Whoever has been given much, much more is expected."*

Now that you know your unique S.H.A.P.E., invest your time, energy, and resources to proving faithful with your talents and multiplying them for God's glory. Stop comparing yourself to others and remember you are a part of a family! Like the 4 D's in the road trip of life, if you take away one of the D's you won't arrive at your destination together. You can have a destination and a drive, but without directions you'll get lost. Take your SHAPE and offer it to God in service to his kingdom!

Day 40: Where Do I Go from Here?

Congratulations, you have made it through "40 Days in the Desert"! Hopefully, in the past 40 days you have begun to develop the critical V.A.L.U.E.S. and H.A.B.I.T.S. of spiritual growth. As you continue your spiritual journey everything you learn will build upon these critical principles. It's important to always continue growing because the moment you stop growing spiritually you start declining spiritually. Keep fighting the good fight and finish the race of faith!

2 Peter 1:5-11
- Why must we add these character traits to my life?
- How do these traits help me when they become a part of my life according to verse 8?
- Verse 10 tells me to do what?

Colossians 3:12-17
- Verse 12 says you are who?
- What are you to put on?
- How are you to treat your brothers and sisters in the Lord? (verse 13)
- What bonds Christians to each other? (verse 14).
- What is to rule my heart each day? (verse 15).

1 Corinthians 6:19-20
- What two things does this passage say about me?
- What has God done for me through Jesus? (verse 20).
- What does God want me to do all the days of my life with this body I live in? (verse 20).
- How do we honor God with our body?

Today's Take Away

1. Pray each day God will help you to make changes in your life to become more like his son, Jesus.

2. Continue reviewing your new values and habits and the scriptures you've memorized, and keep growing in them everyday!

The V.A.L.U.E.S & H.A.B.I.T.S. of Spiritual Growth!

V-alue my relationship w/ God, above all.

A-lways need spiritual encouragement to endure.

L-et God's Word guide my life.

U-nderstand my need for godly training.

E-njoy bringing souls to Christ.

S-incerely care about the needs of others.

H-ave a daily Quiet Time.

A-ttend regular church meetings.

B-iblically memorize and meditate.

I-nvite discipling in my life.

T-ell others the Good News.

S-erve others w/ my S.H.A.P.E.

WEEK 7: *Communicating With God—Listen*
(I) Value my relationship with God, above all.
(Therefore, I) Have a Daily Quiet Time.

Monday

Read 2 Timothy 3:16. Since all scripture is God breathed when we open our Bibles we aren't just studying the words in a textbook. We are actually listening to the very voice of God! How important do you think it is to listen to the words and wisdom of the Creator of the Universe? Read Deuteronomy 8:3. God was teaching Israel that *true life* doesn't come from bread, but rather from the very words that come from the mouth of God. In what ways do you think the word of God gives life? Read 1 Peter 2:2. What do you crave more? Bread or God's Word? Write Matthew 4:4 down on an index card and spend this week memorizing and meditating on it throughout the day.

Tuesday

Too often people read their Bibles, check their quiet time off of their "To Do List" and then don't think about what they read for the rest of the day or week. I know because I've been there and done that. Over the years I've learned, whether my quiet time is 50 minutes or only 5 minutes, to always walk away with a verse and point to memorize and meditate on for the day or week. That is where God truly changes our lives! Read Psalm 119:97-104. Look up the word *meditate* in a dictionary. What does the word meditate mean? What attributes did the psalmist possess as a result of meditating on the word of God? What will meditating on the word of God do for you as a Christian? How might the following scriptures apply to today's lesson? Psalm 19:7-11; 119:105; Romans 15:4. Continue memorizing and meditating on Matthew 4:4.

REMEMBER: IT DOESN'T MATTER HOW SHORT OR LONG YOUR QUIET TIME WITH GOD IS. WHAT REALLY MATTERS IS WHAT YOU WALK AWAY WITH. ALWAYS LEAVE YOUR TIME WITH GOD WITH A VERSE AND POINT TO MEDITATE ON FOR THE DAY/WEEK!

Wednesday

Part of the power of meditating on God's word is that it will transform you. Read Romans 12:1-2. According to verse 2, we will be transformed by what? How do you think meditating on God's Word will renew your mind? By meditating on God's Word we are actually programming our brains to think differently, and when we think differently we will act differently. How might the following scriptures apply to today's lesson? Deuteronomy 6:5-6; Psalm 119:9-11; James 1:21. Continue memorizing and meditating on Matthew 4:4.

Thursday

Sometimes I have a 5 minute quiet time and spend the rest of the day meditating on what I read, but it's also important that I have 50 minute quiet times where I really *study* the word of God. Read 2 Timothy 2:15. How should you present yourself to God? What should you be competent in handling? Do you think you'll become competent by only having 5 minute quiet times? The Word should not only be read, but studied. Pray for wisdom and understanding; ask questions regarding hard-to-understand verses; use cross-references, concordances and other Bible helps to aid in your understanding. How might the following scriptures apply to today's lesson? Acts 17:11 (look up the verb *examine*); 2 Timothy 3:16-17—focus on verse 17; 1 Peter 3:15. Continue memorizing and meditating on Matthew 4:4.

Friday

As you meditate on God's Word, the goal is to move it from your head to your heart to your life. Read James 1:22-25. Is it enough to just study the Bible? What must you do as you learn the Word? Do you find yourself just *hearing* the word of God? If so, what can you do to change that? How might the following scriptures apply to today's lesson? Joshua 1:8; Matthew 7:21-27; John 8:31-32. Continue memorizing and meditating on Matthew 4:4.

Spend the weekend reviewing what you learned this week.

WEEK 8: *Communicating with God—Speak*
(I) Value my relationship with God, above all.
(Therefore, I) Have a Daily Quiet Time.

Monday

When you pray should you say, "Holy Lord God Almighty who dwells in majesty in the heavenly realms?" Or, "Hey Dad, what's up?" I know I've personally wrestled with the idea, "How does God want me to speak to him in prayer?" Read Luke 11:1-4. We find Christ praying when one of his disciples comes along and asks him, *"Lord, teach us to pray..."* This week we are going to spend some time letting the Word teach us how to pray. Take a moment and ask God to use his Word to teach you how he wants you to speak to him in prayer. Read Romans 8:15. According to this verse when we speak to God what are two of the names we "cry out"? Abba is an Aramaic word which means "daddy" or "papa." What sense does the name "Father" give? What sense does the name "Dad/Daddy" give? What Paul is saying is when you are born again (John 3:3-5), you are adopted into God's family. This makes God, both your Father and your Dad. In other words, when you speak to God there is a tension between him as your Father/authority figure and your Dad/affectionate parent. Personally, I always try to balance giving him my respect as my Father yet the affection and informality of a Dad. No matter how you address him according to John 14:13, in whose name do we ask? Write Romans 8:15 down on an index card and spend this week memorizing and meditating on it throughout the day.

Tuesday

Everyday Jesus made time to pray. Not just when he ate or at night before bed, but throughout the day. Read the following: Luke 3:20-21; 5:16; 6:12. How often did Jesus withdraw from his busy day to pray? Where did he go to pray? Do you have a place to pray? Read Matthew 6:5-15. In verse 7, do our prayers have to be very long? Learn to pray 10 second prayers throughout the day. Continue memorizing and meditating on Romans 8:15.

Wednesday

It is important for us to remember who we are addressing. Various positions in prayer reflect the type of prayer and humility we must have before God. Read Ephesians 3:14-15. Paul knew that he was praying to the God of the universe. For this reason he knelt and called him Father. How might the following scriptures apply to today's lesson? Psalm 95:6; Matthew 26:39; Mark 11:25. Continue memorizing and meditating on Romans 8:15.

Thursday

Read Ephesians 6:18. How should we pray? What does it mean to "*pray in the Spirit*"? When should we pray? Write down the kinds of prayers you ought to be praying. Who should you be praying constantly for? Have you been doing this? How might the following scriptures apply to today's lesson? John 17:20-21; Ephesians 3:14-19; James 1:5. Continue memorizing and meditating on Romans 8:15. Contact someone who needs your prayers and pray with them on the phone.

Friday

Does God always answer prayers? Absolutely! It's just that sometimes his answer is "Yes", "No" or "Wait." Learn to trust God whatever his answer is (see Proverbs 3:5). Read James 4:1-3. Prayers are sometimes rejected by God; either they are not in accordance with his divine will (2 Corinthians 12:7-10), or there is a problem with us. From verse 1, what causes fights and arguments? The term "*kill*" in verse 2 is referring to spiritual murder, not physical. Hating our brothers makes us murderers (1 John 3:15). Read Matthew 5:21-23 for further insight. According to James 4:2-3, what two things prevent us from "receiving" from the Lord? Why won't the Lord grant requests asked out of impure motives? Another reason why we don't receive is because we lack persistence (Luke 18:1). Remember to talk to your spiritual dad/father and friend throughout the day. Continue memorizing and meditating on Romans 8:15.

Spend the weekend reviewing what you learned this week.

WEEK 9: *Relationships in Christ*
(I) Always need spiritual encouragement to endure.
(Therefore, I) Attend regular church meetings.

Monday

Last week your memory verse was Romans 8:15, which talked about being adopted into God's family. This week we are going to focus on God's heart and will for his family. Imagine if you had several children at the same school and one of your children was frequently picked on by the school bully. How would you feel if the other children never came to his defense? Never asked him how he was doing? They didn't stick close together so he wasn't such an easy target? Read 1 Peter 5:8-9. Who is the spiritual bully that targets Christians? Who does the lion/Satan attack? The entire herd or the stray animal? In the same way, church isn't some Sunday event you attend just to check off of your spiritual check list. When the church get's together it's like the family gathering together to strengthen each other and protect the weak. Read 1 Corinthians 10:12. What happens when you feel like you're "standing firm" enough where you don't need the church's encouragement? Read Hebrews 10:24-25. Is going to church only about your personal encouragement? What does God want you to do for others? When you don't go to church you are one less person God can use to strengthen others. Write Hebrews 10:24-25 down on an index card and spend this week memorizing and meditating on it throughout the day.

Tuesday

As you saw yesterday, God wants his family to stick together and care for one another. Read John 13:34-35. What kind of heart does God expect his children to have for one another? How does God want you to show your love for his children? The world's love is just a feeling that comes and goes. God's love is agape love, which in greek is action oriented and not just feelings. Read 1 John 3:17-18. How does God want us to love each other? Have you been living out your love for your brothers and sisters? Read 1 Corinthians 13:1-4. Write down the areas of love you think you can grow in? Find ways this week to encourage at least one person everyday. Continue memorizing and meditating on Hebrews 10:24-25.

Wednesday

Today we are going to look at the attitude we should have toward our brothers and sisters in Christ. Read Philippians 2:1-7. According to verse 5 whose attitude should you be imitating? What was Jesus' attitude in verse 7? What should our attitude be like according to verse 3-4? Read Ephesians 5:1-2. Who's love are we called to imitate? When your attitude becomes one of genuine love (action and service oriented love) you can't help it but to express that love to those around you. Carefully consider the attitude present as the brothers and sisters *served* one another in Acts 2:42-47. What were they *devoted* to? What was their attitude towards material things? What was their concern? (verse 45) What is the result of having a *servant's* mindset? (verse 46). Continue memorizing and meditating on Hebrews 10:24-25.

Thursday

Read 1 Peter 1:22. How strong does God want our love to be for one another? Read Hebrews 3:12-13. How often should we express that love? Why? Today I want you to spend time writing a list of disciples you think you can encourage. Write down how you can encourage them. Finally, pray for each person and ask God to increase your love for them and his church. Continue memorizing and meditating on Hebrews 10:24-25.

Friday

Read Romans 12:9-21. In your notes write down all of the different ways these verses show we should love one another. When you are done pick two things that you think you could grow in the most. Write down how you think you could start living out those two things today. Continue memorizing and meditating on Hebrews 10:24-25.

Spend the weekend reviewing what you learned this week.

WEEK 10: Sunday Worship
*(I) Always need spiritual encouragement to endure.
(Therefore, I) Attend regular church meetings.*

Monday

How do churches decide what to do for their Sunday Worship? Read Ephesians 2:19-20. What should be the foundation on which we build the church? Where do we find what the apostles and prophets taught? Let's spend the rest of the week finding out what the Bible says about our time together on Sunday. Read Luke 22:7-10. What were Jesus and his disciples getting ready to celebrate? Look up *Passover* in a Bible dictionary. What does the bread represent? How about the fruit of the vine? Read 1 Corinthians 11:23-26. Why are we repeating this ceremony still today? Write down and think about what goes through your mind when you take the bread and the fruit of the vine on Sunday. Read Acts 20:7. Secular history also points out that it was the practice of the early church to partake of the Lord's Supper every Sunday. Write Ephesians 2:19-20 down on an index card and spend this week memorizing and meditating on it each the day. Let the Bible be the foundation of everything you do.

Tuesday

Why do churches take up a collection of money on Sundays? Read 1 Corinthians 16:1-3. In verse 3, their contribution was a gift to who? The Jerusalem church was struggling financially and needed help so the Corinthian church collected money to help meet their needs. Are there still needs today? Do you think we should still meet them? (See the heart of the church in Acts 2:45). Read 2 Corinthians 9:6-15. What kind of giver does God want you to be? Look at verse 12-13, how is giving described? Should you plan ahead to set aside funds to give on Sunday? Continue memorizing and meditating on Ephesians 2:19-20.

Wednesday

Read James 5:16. Many people go to Sunday Worship dressed up and try to present themselves as "put together."

According to this verse does God want us to go to church and pretend everything is fine when it is not? What does God call us to do when there are sins in our life that we are struggling with? To whom should you confess your sins? What is the purpose of confessing your sins? Read Proverbs 28:13. What happens if you don't confess your sins? What happens when you do? Confessing sin and not being ashamed before the Lord is necessary for effective and powerful prayer. Continue memorizing and meditating on Ephesians 2:19-20. Find a sister/brother and confess your sins and pray for each other.

Thursday

Another area of worship is singing. Read Ephesians 5 and Colossians 3 carefully and write down the key attitudes necessary to become filled with God's Spirit. Let's focus on Ephesians 5:17-21. What does getting drunk on wine lead to? What does being "filled" with the Holy Spirit lead to? The **result** of being filled with the Spirit is a joyful heart that **sings**. Notice how these verses aren't talking about Sunday worship, but rather a lifestyle of joyful song. Sunday is just a continuation of this. Read 1 Corinthians 14:15. What does God want you to sing with? God does not judge the quality of your voice, but rather the quality of your heart! What do you usually sing with? Continue memorizing and meditating on Ephesians 2:19-20.

Friday

Hopefully, after this week you'll see the Sunday worship in a whole new light. Isn't it amazing how God has laid a foundation that is designed to encourage and build up his church? Read Ephesians 4:11-16. Why has God assigned apostles, prophets, evangelists, teachers and pastors to the church? Look up each word online (blueletterbible.com). Why is it important to grow? Notice verses 15 and 16: What is your part in church growth? What can you do to prepare yourself for the works of service in the church? Write down your thoughts on Jeremiah 18:1-6. Continue memorizing and meditating on Ephesians 2:19-20.

Spend the weekend reviewing what you learned this week.

WEEK 11: Dying to Self and Living for Christ
(I) Let God's Word Guide my Life.
(Therefore, I) Biblically Memorize and Meditate.

Monday

Being a Christian doesn't mean that the evil desires you had in the past are now magically gone. So how do you deal with those evil desires that are still in you? Read Luke 9:23-27. What happens on a cross? What do you think it means to take up one's cross? It means trying to put the evil desires in your life to death (see Colossians 3:5). So how do you put your old desires to death? Read Ephesians 4:17-19. According to verse 19, can you lose your sensitivity to sin? When you give your evil desires what they want they have a continual hunger for more. The key to putting sin to death is to starve it to death. Don't feed it even a little. In what ways do you feed the evil desires in your life? Make a list of the areas: ungodly movies, books, music, conversations, relationships, etc., that you are feeding to your sin. Share it with another disciple and ask for prayers. Write Luke 9:23 down on an index card and spend this week memorizing and meditating on it throughout the day.

Tuesday

A struggle that every Christian has is trying to hold onto an old way of life and still follow Christ. By holding on to your old way of life you make living for Christ a painful process, when it should be a joy to live for Christ. Read Philippians 3:7-8. What was Paul's attitude about his old life? How did Paul feel about his knowledge of Christ? How do you view your Christian life? Are you happy to be a Christian? Paul clearly saw that it is better to be a Christian than be a sinner. Can you say the same thing about yourself? Continue memorizing and meditating on Luke 9:23. Get together with a brother/sister and pray to depend totally on God and not on anything in the world.

Wednesday

Read Ephesians 4:22-24. From these verses we can see two

main points. The first point being that the old self must be put off. The scriptures teach that our old self was corrupted by its deceitful desires. We need to treat our old self as old clothes that we are ashamed to be seen in. The second point is that the new self must be put on. Romans 13:14 says to clothe yourself with Christ. What type of clothes are you wearing? Continue memorizing and meditating on Luke 9:23.

Thursday

When we were baptized in Christ, we were baptized into his death and resurrection to live for righteousness and not for sin. Being baptized meant that the old self was no longer going to live, but to die. If our old ways are *dead*, then we have no reason to look back on our old life, since we have died to it. Examine Luke 9:57-62. In verse 62 Jesus says, *"No one who puts his hand to the plow and looks back is fit for service in the Kingdom of God."* What does Christ mean by "looking back"? If you're plowing a field and decide to look back while plowing, would you still be able to plow a straight line? Now examine your own life. Is it possible to live a godly life and yet desire the worldly life you once had? Continue memorizing and meditating on Luke 9:23.

Friday

What type attitude does an Olympic athlete have in regards to obtaining a gold medal? What must they do in order to win? Examine Philippians 3:12-14. As Christ servants we set our goals to be what Christ wants us to be. We should let Christ direct our steps and not us direct Christ's steps. From verse 13 we can see that we need to forget about our sinful past and look forward to what is ahead. In the end, after pressing on toward the goal, we can all share in the reward of everlasting life. Continue memorizing and meditating on Luke 9:23. Call a brother or sister and encourage them to press on towards the goal of love, just as Paul encouraged us.

Spend the weekend reviewing what you learned this week.

WEEK 12: Should I Follow My Heart?
(I) Let God's Word Guide my Life.
(Therefore, I) Biblically Memorize and Meditate.

Monday

Read 1 Samuel 16:7. What does man look at? What does God look at? What does it mean that God looks at our heart? Read 1 Corinthians 4:5. What in the heart will God expose? The heart is where our motivation comes from. Read 1 Corinthians 13:1-8. Can we do the right thing with the wrong motives? In verses 1-3, how does God view our actions when our motives are wrong? Write Jeremiah 17:9 down on an index card and spend this week memorizing and meditating on it throughout the day. The world encourages us to follow our heart, but what does God say about following our feelings?

Tuesday

The world says follow your heart. What does God say that we should follow? Read Jeremiah 17:9-10. What is the most deceitful thing? Can you trust your feelings to tell you what is right and what is wrong? How often does the way you feel change? Does God want you to build your life on something that changes so much? What does God want you to build your life on instead? Read Matthew 7:24-28. Does God's Word ever change? God wants you to build your life on the solid rock of his Word. Our motivations are naturally selfish. In fact, the majority of our sins come from the evil desires of the heart (see Mark 7:20-23). Who can clean up our heart? Read Psalm 51:10. Continue memorizing and meditating on Jeremiah 17:9. Take time today to pray with a friend for a pure heart.

Wednesday

When you were baptized you received the gift of the Holy Spirit (see Acts 2:38), and God's Spirit can work through your heart to convict you of sin. Read 1 John 3:19-24. As you mature spiritually you will to be able to better decipher whether your heart is motivating you towards God's will or Satan's. Read

Hebrews 3:12-13. What will a sinful, unbelieving heart do? What must you do to prevent your heart from hardening? In verse 13, how does God describe sin? Since sin and the heart are so deceitful it's so important that we have other Christians in our lives to help encourage us to not become hard hearted or deceived. Continue memorizing and meditating on Jeremiah 17:9. Call a friend from church today and talk about any sins that have been deceiving you and hardening your heart.

Thursday

Because the heart is at the root of the problem, this is the place where God does his work in the individual. For instance, the work of the law is "written in their hearts," and conscience is the proof of this (Romans 2:14-15). The heart is the field where the seed (the Word of God) is sown (Matthew 13:19; Luke 8:15). In addition to being the place where the natural laws of God are written, the heart is the place of renewal. Reflect upon Titus 3:5-6. Are you saved by what you do? By whom have you been renewed? (also see John 3:3-6). Now read Colossians 3:9-10. *Why* should we be truthful? How are we renewed? Continue memorizing and meditating on Jeremiah 17:9.

Friday

As we discussed on Wednesday the heart is the dwelling place of God. The Spirit of the living God lives in the heart of the believer. God has given us the *"Spirit in our hearts, as a deposit..."* (2 Corinthians 1:22). Ephesians 3:17 expresses the desire that *"Christ may dwell in your hearts by faith."* The love of God *"is shed abroad in our hearts by the Holy Spirit which is given unto us"* (Romans 5:5). The job of the Holy Spirit has always been to create since the beginning of the world. Now his job is to re-create you from the inside out. He orders our life, gives it a purpose and meaning, and helps it to make sense. He's good at it. Let him do it. Read 2 Chronicles 16:9. What will God find when he searches your heart? Continue memorizing and meditating on Jeremiah 17:9.

Spend the weekend reviewing what you learned this week.

WEEK 13: *Let Others Help You*
(I) Understand my need for godly training.
(Therefore, I) Invite discipling in my life.

Monday

Read Jeremiah 18:2-6. Based on these verses why do you think the Lord sent Jeremiah to the potter's house? How is it that we can be like clay in the Lord's hand? When a clay sculpture hasn't become hard yet and it's still moldable, an artist can slowly work out any imperfections until it's just the way they want. How does God want you to look? If you want to continue to grow and stay faithful till the end you must develop a moldable heart. Read Roman 8:28-29. God is using everything in our lives to conform us to whose likeness? Having a moldable heart starts with understanding that you have sins and imperfections that God wants to work out of your life (see Ezekiel 7:20). This week we will examine the various tools God uses to mold you into the image of Christ, and the heart you need to have. Write Proverbs 27:17 down on an index card and spend this week memorizing and meditating on it throughout the day.

Tuesday

According to this week's memory verse Proverbs 27:17, what is one tool God will use to mold you? Therefore what should your attitude be when another Christian points something out in your life that needs to be corrected? One of the hardest things about being moldable is having the humility to accept input from others. When someone tries to correct you, how do you usually respond? Do you show your annoyance at once (see Proverbs 12:16)? Do you turn away from discipline, or seek it knowing it will help you become more like Christ (Proverbs 15:5)? Continue memorizing and meditating on Proverbs 27:17.

Wednesday

Often times the problem we have with correction isn't with what's being said, but *how* it's being said. Read Ephesians 4:2-3. According to this verse how should we bear with one another in love? In verse 3 what is the goal when being humble and gentle towards one another? Remember, it isn't just receiving input with humility, but it's also about giving input to others with humility, gentleness and great patience. Read 2 Timothy 2:24-26. According to verse 25, how should you correct those around you? Whose job is it ultimately to get people's heart ready to repent? Read Hebrews 10:24. Are you considering how you can help others become more like Jesus? Continue memorizing and meditating on Proverbs 27:17.

Thursday
Read Proverbs 11:14. What happens when there is a lack of guidance in your life? How many advisers should you have in your life? What happens when you have many advisers? Read Proverbs 27:5-6. What do you think "hidden love" means? What do you think it means when a friend just "multiplies kisses"? Therefore, who are the true friends in your life that you should trust? Read 2 Corinthians 7:10-11. Does some advice hurt or cause you sorrow? What do you think is the difference between worldly and godly sorrow? What does sorrow of the world lead to? What does godly sorrow lead to? What other attitudes does godly sorrow produce? Stay pliable even when it's uncomfortable. Continue memorizing and meditating on Proverbs 27:17.

Friday
At the end of the day always remember that when you receive correction the final decision whether or not to apply it is still yours. Don't just blindly do whatever other Christians say. Read Philippians 2:12. Whose responsibility is it to work out your salvation? No one else is responsible for your final salvation but you. Read Philippians 1:9-10. Sometimes people will give you good advice, but verse 10 says that it's up to you to discern if it is what? Stay humble and pliable, but develop the character to discern what is true and best. Continue memorizing and meditating on Proverbs 27:17.

Spend the weekend reviewing what you learned this week.

WEEK 14: Rabbi Jesus and Discipleship
(I) Understand my need for godly training.
(Therefore, I) Invite discipling in my life.

Monday

Read Matthew 28:18-20. This week we are going to look at what it meant to be a disciple in Jesus' day, and how that applies to us today. The term "disciple" was a Jewish term describing a follower's relationship to his Rabbi. Jesus is our Jewish Rabbi (Ravi=My Master). Read Matthew 11:28-30. A Rabbi was a special teacher of God's law who tried to figure out how to apply God's commands in his day and age. Their list of teachings were called a "yoke." The Rabbi chose disciples (followers) who he felt could live out the commands the same way he did. A disciple was someone who tried to live like his Rabbi. In verse 28, how many people does Jesus say can "come to me" and be like me? In verse 30 does Jesus say that his yoke is complicated and too hard to follow? In verse 29, what do you find when learning to live like Jesus? Discipleship is all about living like our Rabbi Jesus (see 1 John 2:6). Write James 5:26 down on an index card and spend this week memorizing and meditating on it throughout the day.

Tuesday

Read Matthew 5:17. When a Rabbi felt you were applying God's Word correctly to your life he said, "You have fulfilled the law." When he didn't he said, "You have abolished the law." The Rabbi and his disciples were constantly involved in one another's lives in order to help each other "fulfill the law." Do you have other Christians consistently involved in your life? Are you willing to allow them to hold you accountable to carrying Jesus' yoke? For the rest of this week I want you to examine how "accountability" is key to living like Jesus. Find "accountable"in the dictionary. Read Hebrews 4:12-13. According to this verse who is really uncovering our hearts? What, then, does God use to hold us accountable to him? Continue memorizing and meditating on James 5:16.

Wednesday

One of the best examples of discipleship is Ezekiel 33:7-11. What role is Ezekiel given? Isn't this the same role that disciples are given in one another's lives (especially leaders)? What will happen to leaders if they don't warn you about your sin? What happens to you if you listen to what they warn you about? What happens if you don't listen? Remember, we can't help each other if we don't know what's going on in each other's lives. Confession is the doorway into our souls. Continue memorizing and meditating on James 5:16. Make a list of things you can confess to a brother or sister this week. Be open to their advice and direction.

Thursday

Accountability is a word we tend to shy away from. Why do you think that is? Read Romans 14:12-13. Is accountability about judging one another? Is it about telling others what they have to do? Remember Hebrews 4, it's not our personal opinions that judge, but the word of God! Read Romans 15:1-8. In verse 4, does accountability mean you point out every single weakness you see in others? Are we to mainly use the scriptures to hurt or encourage one another? Discipleship is not a forum for judgment, but for training in righteousness out of love for each other. Continue memorizing and meditating on James 5:16.

Friday

The key to remember this week is that the goal of discipleship is about trying to be more like Jesus. Read Hebrews 12:5-16. In verses 8, what happens when you don't have anyone in your life to help discipline you? In verse 11, does discipline always feel good? In the end, what does discipline do for those who have been trained by it? Remember, Matthew 11:28-30, is Jesus yoke given to burden us? No! It's designed to set us free from the burden of sin (remember Ezekiel 33:7-11?). In verses 14-15, what is the final goal of holiness? To see the Lord. Continue memorizing and meditating on James 5:16.

Spend the weekend reviewing what you learned this week.

WEEK 15: Sharing My Faith
(I) Enjoy bringing souls to Christ.
(Therefore, I) Tell others the good news.

Monday

Read 2 Corinthians 5:9. What should our goal in life be? Are you driven more to please God or people? Read 2 Corinthians 5:10-21. According to these verses what absolutely pleases God? God wants his lost children home. Whose ambassador are you? What ministry has God given to us? On whose behalf are you speaking? Develop the heart that wants to please God by bringing souls to Christ. Write Philemon 6 down on an index card and spend this week memorizing and meditating on it throughout the day. Realize that the more you share your faith, the more understanding you will gain of every good thing you have in Jesus. What kind of attitude do you think this understanding will produce? Thankfulness? Boldness? Humility? Call a friend in the church and go evangelizing with them this week.

Tuesday

We have all been given an eternal mission to rescue souls from darkness. Have you truly embraced God's call for you to be an ambassador to a lost and dying world? Read Matthew 28:18-20. What did Jesus command his disciples to do? What does Jesus command you to do today? Read Luke 9:23-26. What must you do in order to follow Jesus? What will happen if you are ashamed of Jesus? Being ashamed often has to do with low self-esteem. In Christ, our esteem is redeemed through him and strengthened because of his Spirit. We belong to him and he reassures us as his sons (remember Hebrews 12:5-ff). Read Ephesians 1:7-8. Reflect on the things that God has lavished upon you. Look up "lavish" in a dictionary. Share God's message of reconciliation with someone at work today. Continue memorizing and meditating on Philemon 6.

Wednesday

I've never met a person who doesn't at times struggle with the fear of talking to people about Jesus. Boldness is something everyone has to grow in. Some more than others. Read Romans 1:16-17. Why was Paul not ashamed of the gospel? What is the gospel? (See 1 Corinthians 15:3-4). Of what kind of importance is the gospel? Why? Read Acts 4:29-31. How often do you pray for boldness to share the gospel? Think of someone today that you want to share the gospel with. Pray for boldness and go share with that person what Christ has done for you. Continue memorizing and meditating on Philemon 6.

Thursday

In John 12:49, Jesus reveals that how you say something might be just as important as what you say. Read Philippians 2:14-15. What kind of attitude should you maintain in every situation? Why? Read 1 Peter 3:15-16. How should you answer those that question you about your beliefs? What do you think it means to set Christ apart in your heart as Lord? We all talk about what's in our hearts the most. When Christ occupies the highest place in your heart it becomes natural to talk about him whenever you have the opportunity. This is important because the easiest and most tactful way to share your faith is when it is done naturally. Continue memorizing and meditating on Philemon 6.

Friday

With a heart to please God, and with boldness and tactfulness, you will become an amazing ambassador for Christ. Read 1 Corinthians 9:20-23. What was Paul willing to do in order to just save a few people? Have you ever led anyone to Christ? If so, what are some things that you have done to help them get saved? Think about different ways in which you can give yourself to reach people that you come in contact with every day. Read Ephesians 2:10. What does it mean that God prepares things in advance for you to do? Start praying for God to set up appointments for you to share your faith with people who are seeking him. Continue memorizing and meditating on Philemon 6.

Spend the weekend reviewing what you learned this week.

WEEK 16: *Proclaiming Christ*
(I) Enjoy bringing souls to Christ.
(Therefore, I) Tell others the good news.

Monday

Last week we talked about sharing our faith and teaching the gospel with boldness. How have you been doing? What are some things that might hold you back? Read Matthew 10:32-33. In verse 33, if you don't "confess" or "acknowledge" Christ, what are you, in fact, doing? Remember Romans 1:16, don't be ashamed of Christ. Would you speak to others about Jesus more often if you were encouraged by a brother or sister? Call another disciple and ask him or her to challenge you in this area. Read 1 John 4:15. Put this task to work today. Invite people to church today and tell them about Christ. Write Matthew 28:19-20 down on an index card and spend this week memorizing and meditating on it throughout the day.

Tuesday

Read Mark 5:18-20. What kind of attitude did this man have after his deliverance? Why did Jesus object to his following him? What did Jesus call him to do? Why did Jesus tell him to do this? What did this man do as a result of Jesus' instructions? To whom must you confess Christ? Read Matthew 5:13-16. What does salt and light do? Make a list of 1) ways you are now impacting others for Christ, 2) additional ways you could be impacting others for Christ. If you don't confess Christ, you become like a lamp hidden under a bowl. Think of three people you can impact today and go let your light shine on them. Continue memorizing and meditating on Matthew 28:19-20.

Wednesday

Read Acts 24:24-25. What did Paul speak to Felix and his wife about? What three things did his message include? Why did you think Felix became afraid? Will the gospel be accepted by everyone? What must you teach people when confessing Christ? Read 2 Corinthians 5:10-11. What must others need to know when we share the Lord with them? What is the motivation to tell others of Christ? Is it a serious matter for others to know? Why? How motivated are you in telling others of Jesus? Read James 5:20. Speak to someone today about the hope of the good news. Continue memorizing and meditating on the Great Commission in Matthew 28:19-20.

Thursday

Read Hebrews 10:38-39. What happens when you shrink back from letting your like shine? We tend to shrink back when we forget what God has done for us. Read Psalm 145:8-12. Describe the person of God as taught by the psalmist? Why are his saints excited in the Lord? What great things has the Lord done for you personally? What mighty acts has he done in your life? How has he been gracious to you? How has he been compassionate to you? How has he been patient with you today? How has he richly loved you? Should what God has done for you motivate you to shrink back or let your light shine? Tell someone today about the kingdom of Christ and what he's done in your life. Continue memorizing and meditating on Matthew 28:19-20.

Friday

Learn to love what God loves! That's bringing his lost children home! Read 1 Peter 3:15. What does it mean to *set apart Christ as Lord?* What's in your heart and what do you care the most about? What do your actions show that you care the most about? When Christ is what you care the most about what will you do when you meet someone who is lost? As you share how can you prepare yourself to answer those who question your faith? Write down some ways you can prepare yourself for this task? How should we answer everyone? As time goes on, you can learn evidences for God and the Bible, and how to deal with atheists, agnostics, and people of other "faiths." Prepare yourself and God will use you in many ways. Continue memorizing and meditating on Matthew 28:19-20. Until Christ comes let your light shine so that those in darkness can find their way home!

Spend the weekend reviewing what you learned this week.

WEEK 17: *The Greatest in the Kingdom*
(I) Sincerely care about the needs of others.
(Therefore, I) Serve others with my S.H.A.P.E.

Monday

Read Matthew 20:25-28. Who is the greatest in the kingdom of Heaven? Who will be first amongst all of God's children? How close are you to being #1? What makes someone great in God's eyes is totally different than in the world. What did Jesus come into the world to do? When you are around the church family do you usually look to serve or be served? Make a list of ways that you can serve others in the kingdom and in your neighborhood. Don't wait, start serving today. Write Mark 10:45 down on an index card and spend this week memorizing and meditating on it throughout the day. Get together with another Christian and find someone you can serve this week.

Tuesday

Read Colossians 3:23-24 and Ephesians 6:7-8. When you do anything, who is it that you should be doing it for? Do you feel like most of the things you currently do are to please God, yourself or others? *How* should you serve or work? In what ways could you be a better example of Christ at your job? When you wake up each day, pray that you may please the Lord in all that you do. Renew your mind with the Bible and become a servant. Call a disciple and ask them how you can serve them today. Continue memorizing and meditating on Mark 10:45.

Wednesday

Read Philippians 2:3-8. Whom should you consider as better than yourself? Whose interests should you protect? Whose attitude should you have? What is that attitude? Would others describe you as a humble person? Read Philippians 2:14-15. Believe that you can make a difference in this crooked and perverse generation. Get together with a close friend and pray to make a difference at your workplace for the glory of God. Do something for someone at your workplace or school who doesn't get along with you. Show them love by what you do, and believe that the Lord is using you. Continue memorizing and meditating on Mark 10:45.

Thursday

Read Luke 17:7-10. As Christ's servant, when you have done everything you were told to do, what should be your attitude? Do you ever feel like you deserve something after you serve, like praise, thanks, or some reward? Read Galatians 1:10. What happens when you serve to win the approval from anyone but God? Convince yourself of these words and realize that whatever you do will be seen by God. Are you currently involved in any ministry that is serving others? If not, think of a ministry you can join or volunteer for where you serve others and glorify God with your example. Continue memorizing and meditating on Mark 10:45.

Friday

When all is said and done, serving is truly about humility. Are you really willing to put others before yourself? There's a great acronym that helps remind me of the attitude Christ wants me to have. **J.O.Y.** Jesus. Others. (and then) Yourself. Read John 13:12-17. What does Jesus do at his last supper with the disciples? What was Jesus trying to teach his disciples by washing their feet? Would you ever wash someone else's feet? If not, why? If Jesus would, but you wouldn't, what do you think that tells you about yourself as compared to Jesus? If not literally, how have you "washed" other people's feet? What attitudes have prevented you from freely giving yourself to serve your spouse, coworker, family member, friend, neighbor, or children? Learn to serve without being asked...as working for the Lord and not for men...in order to please God and bring Him glory! Continue memorizing and meditating on Mark 10:45.

Spend the weekend reviewing what you learned this week.

WEEK 18: Let Your Light Shine
(I) Sincerely care about the needs of others.
(Therefore, I) Serve others with my S.H.A.P.E.

Monday

Read James 2:14-18. Is it enough just to *know* what to do? Is it enough just to intellectually believe? What happens if your faith is not accompanied by deeds (actions)? How is your faith manifested before men? Read verses 19-24. In verse 22, when what Abraham's faith made complete? In what areas of your life has your faith and deeds *not* been working together? Write Ephesians 2:10 down on an index card and spend this week memorizing and meditating on it throughout the day. Remember: we are not saved by faith *plus* works, but by a faith *that* works. Pray everyday for God to set up appointments for you to do good works!

Tuesday

Read Matthew 5:16. How is your example at work? If your coworkers don't know that you are a Christian would they be surprised to hear that you are one? Why or why not? In this verse should it be a surprise that you are a disciple of Christ? What is the purpose of letting your life shine before your coworkers? To glorify yourself? Read Romans 13:12. Don't just stick to doing your job at work; remember to do the Lord's work at your job. Get to know someone at work or school that you haven't met before. See to it that your light shines to guide them to the Lord. Continue memorizing and meditating on Ephesians 2:10.

Wednesday

Most of us are constantly in contact with people at work, at the grocery store, at school, on the road, and even online. What kind of impression do you make? Do you impress yourself upon them or do you impress *Jesus* upon them? Study out 2 Corinthians 4:5. Do you tend to be a self-promoter? According to this verse, how should you present yourself to others? Would people in your life refer to you as a servant? Remember Jesus came to serve, not to be served. Read 2 Corinthians 5:14-15. What motivated Paul in life? What should Christ's love motivate you to stop doing and start doing? Are you still living for yourself or for Christ? Make it goal today to be a slave to everyone around you. Continue memorizing and meditating on Ephesians 2:10.

Thursday

How does your light shine around other believers? Read John 13:34-35. If our love for other disciples is the test of our faithfulness would you pass or fail? How about your love for other disciples that you feel have hurt you? Read 1 John 2:9-11. Can you possibly be in the light and hate your brother? Read Matthew 5:43-48. Have you "written off" any brother or sister in Christ? Is there anyone you don't greet anymore because of something you have left unresolved? Do you think that pleases God? What should you do immediately? As a disciple are you looking to serve or be served? Encourage or be encouraged? Let God use you to build up another disciple today. Continue memorizing and meditating on Ephesians 2:10.

Friday

Another test of true discipleship is how your light shines at home. You might live with unbelieving parents, or an unbelieving spouse, and children. Whatever the situation, these people see you in your best and worst moments. If it's tough to be a disciple when everything is great, imagine, then, when you're not feeling well? How do you let your "light" shine when you're sick? When you're depressed? When you're angry? When you're stressed? Read again Matthew 5:14-15. Jesus first compares you to a city on a hill, a light for those who are far away, to attract them to the Lord. Next however, he compares you to a light that someone uses in a house. How does your life shine at home? Ask those in your house today what they think of your example. What do you need to change? Continue memorizing and meditating on Ephesians 2:10.

Spend the weekend reviewing what you learned this week.

Now that you've learned the V.A.L.U.E.S. & H.A.B.I.T.S. of spiritual growth it's important to immerse yourself into God's Word and see for yourself how Jesus and his disciples taught and lived those values and habits throughout the New Testament. The following is a schedule to read the entire New Testament in three months by taking 15 minutes a day and reading on average three chapters a day for ninety days. The goal isn't to study all of the details, but rather to get a general overview of the entire N.T.

6 Quick Tips for Bible Reading

1. Begin by asking for God's help and end by praying A.C.T.S.
2. Don't worry about understanding and remembering everything you read.
3. At the end of each chapter write in a notebook what you think is the main point.
4. If you have any questions write them down and ask an older Christian at a later time.
5. Write down how you think today's reading can help you in your new values and habits.
6. Pick one verse each week from your reading to memorize and meditate on.

1. ❑ Matthew 1-4	11. ❑ Acts 4-6
2. ❑ Matthew 5-7	12. ❑ Acts 7-9.
3. ❑ Matthew 8-10	13. ❑ Acts 10-12.
4. ❑ Matthew 11-13	14. ❑ Acts 13-15
5. ❑ Matthew 14-16	15. ❑ Acts 16-18
6. ❑ Matthew 17-19	16. ❑ Acts 19-21:36
7. ❑ Matthew 20-22	17. ❑ Acts 21:37-25:22
8. ❑ Matthew 23-25	18. ❑ Acts 25:23-28:30
9. ❑ Matthew 26-28	19. ❑ Mark 1-3
10. ❑ Acts 1-3	20. ❑ Mark 4-6

21. ❑ Mark 7-9
22. ❑ Mark 10-12
23. ❑ Mark 13-16
24. ❑ 1 Peter 1-3:7
25. ❑ 1 Peter 3:8-5
26. ❑ 2 Peter 1-3
27. ❑ James 1-3:12
28. ❑ James 3:13-5
29. ❑ Luke 1-3
30. ❑ Luke 4-6
31. ❑ Luke 7-9
32. ❑ Luke 10-12
33. ❑ Luke 13-15
34. ❑ Luke 16-18
35. ❑ Luke 19-21
36. ❑ Luke 22-24
37. ❑ 1 Thessalonians 1-3
38. ❑ 1 Thessalonians 4-5
39. ❑ 2 Thessalonians 1-3
40. ❑ 1 Corinthians 1-4
41. ❑ 1 Corinthians 5-7
42. ❑ 1 Corinthians 8-11
43. ❑ 1 Corinthians 12-14
44. ❑ 1 Corinthians 15-16
45. ❑ 2 Corinthians 1-3
46. ❑ 2 Corinthians 4-6
47. ❑ 2 Corinthians 7-9
48. ❑ 2 Corinthians 1-13
49. ❑ Revelation 1-3
50. ❑ Revelations 4-6
51. ❑ Revelations 7-9
52. ❑ Revelation 10-12
53. ❑ Revelations 13-15
54. ❑ Revelation 16-18
55. ❑ Revelation 19-22
56. ❑ Romans 1-3 40

57. ❑ Romans 4-6
58. ❑ Romans7-8
59. ❑ Romans 9-11
60. ❑ Romans 12-13
61. ❑ Romans 14-16
62. ❑ Galatians 1-2
63. ❑ Galatians 3-4
64. ❑ Galatians 5-6:4
65. ❑ Ephesians 1-3
66. ❑ Ephesians 4-6
67. ❑ Philippians 1-2
68. ❑ Philippians 3-4
69. ❑ Colossians 1-2
70. ❑ Colossians 3-4
71. ❑ Philemon
72. ❑ Hebrews 1-2
73. ❑ Hebrews 3-4:13
74. ❑ Hebrews 4:14-7
75. ❑ Hebrews 8-10
76. ❑ Hebrews 11-13
77. ❑ 1 Timothy 1-3
78. ❑ 1 Timothy 4-6
79. ❑ 2 Timothy 1-4
80. ❑ Titus 1-3 2
81. ❑ John 1-3
82. ❑ John 4-6
83. ❑ John 7-9
84. ❑ John 10-12
85. ❑ John 13-16
86. ❑ John 16.5-18
87. ❑ John 19-21
88. ❑ 1 John 1-3:10
89. ❑ 1 John 3-11-5
90. ❑ 2 John; 3 John; Jude

WEEK 33: *God Above All*
(I) Value my relationship with God, above all.
(Therefore, I) Have a Daily Quiet Time.

Monday
Read Matthew 22:37-38. What is the greatest command in the entire Bible? What does it mean to love God will your *all*? Is there anything you hold higher in your heart than God? Is there anything that occupies your mind more than God and godly things? If there anything you put more effort and strength into than your relationship with God? Does God love you with anything less? Read Romans 8:32. Has God held anything back from you? Take time to pray and tell God all of the reasons why he is the greatest thing in your life. Write Matthew 6:33 down on an index card and spend this week memorizing and meditating on it throughout the day.

Tuesday
Read Philippians 3:7-9. Is there anything that compares to your relationship with Jesus? Have you gotten rid of situations, jobs, or other distractions that hinder you from knowing Jesus? Read Luke 8:14. What is preventing this seed from maturing? Can you identify times in your life when distractions hindered you from maturing in your faith and your relationship with God? What is currently in your life that fights for your devotion to God? Now read Matthew 18:7-9. What attitude does Jesus teach you to have about things that cause you to loose your focus? Isn't this a radical way of looking at things? But isn't this the same thing that Paul is saying in the first passage you looked at today? Write down anything you feel you are putting before God and pray for God's strength to give it up. Continue memorizing and meditating on Matthew 6:33.

Wednesday
Read Exodus 20:3. This is the first of the ten commandments. Is there anything that we should put before God? When it comes to your daily time with God, is there anything you put before

him? When it comes to worshipping God at church services is there anything you put before God? Consider King Asa in 2 Chronicles 16:6-13. From verse 8, was Asa accustomed to relying on the Lord? What happened later in his life? What happened to his zeal? Look at Hanani's point in verse 9. Now read Romans 12:9-21. These encouraging snippets all come from a heart that is fully committed to the Lord and not lacking in zeal (verse 11). Our zeal and devotion to Jesus must be consistent. Ask God to empower you to love him with everything you have and make him your closest friend. Continue memorizing and meditating on Matthew 6:33.

Thursday

Read Luke 14:25-35. The word "hate" here in greek literally means love less (see Mark 10:37). Is it acceptable to God with you loving anything or anyone more than him? Can you really be a disciple of Christ if there is anything that you put before your relationship with God? Make a list of the things that you are the most passionate about in life. Rank them in order of importance. Now rank them in order of your time commitment. Do you see any conflicts? Share this with another disciple and ask them to hold you to be accountable in getting your priorities in their correct order. Continue memorizing and meditating on Matthew 6:33.

Friday

In Hebrews 12:18-29, we see an image of when God gave Moses the Ten Commandments. Read through these verses and ask yourself, "What do I see about God in these verses?" Does it seem like he wants to play a special and holy part in our lives? Does he expect to be feared and revered as no other? With that in mind what does verse 28 call you to do? Does your life reflect a reverence and awe for God? Remember to have a healthy fear of God as your Father, but also to keep the tenderness of God as your Dad (see Romans 8:15). Continue memorizing and meditating on Matthew 6:33.

Spend the weekend reviewing what you learned this week.

WEEK 34: Living to Please God
(I) Value my relationship with God, above all.
(Therefore, I) Have a Daily Quiet Time.

Monday

Whose will is the strongest in your heart? God's or your own? Read John 4:34-38. What did Jesus want to fill himself with? From verses 35-38, what do you suppose is the work God that he wants us to finish? Did Jesus put the work of God (will of God) on the back-burner? Let's see how Jesus accomplished completing the will of the Father. Read John 5:30. Could Jesus do it on his own? The confidence Jesus radiated lay in the fact that he sought his Father's will and not his own. Write 2 Corinthians 5:9 down on an index card and spend this week memorizing and meditating on it throughout the day. Start asking yourself in everything you do, "Does this please God?"

Tuesday

Read Mark 14:32-36. When Jesus was in the Garden of Gethsemane was he more focused on pleasing himself or his Father? In verse 36, what was the first thing Jesus acknowledged? Since God is in control and everything is possible for him, doesn't it make sense to surrender everything to him? Even thought Jesus made a plea for himself, he remained subjected to the will of the Father. Jesus is the perfect example of a life that is devoted to pleasing God. Read Hebrews 10:38-39. Even when things were frightening, did Jesus shrink back from pleasing God? Should you? Continue memorizing and meditating on 2 Corinthians 5:9.

Wednesday

Read Ephesians 5:15-21. This is a great list of things that please God. What are some of the things in these verses that you are currently doing to please God? What are some of the things you aren't doing? Notice how it all starts with the heart to find out God's will. Do you constantly ask yourself, "What does God want me to do in this situation? What would please him right now?" Paul says that being a good steward of your time and opportunities pleases God. Not getting drunk pleases God. Being filled with his Spirit pleases God. Singing praises pleases God. Speaking to one another about scripture pleases God. Being grateful about your blessings pleases God. Does your life please God? Is it your life's goal to please God? Continue memorizing and meditating on 2 Corinthians 5:9.

Thursday

Acknowledging God in the way you think and speak is a testimony toward a dedication to please him. Read carefully James 4:13-17. How does James teach that you should acknowledge Jesus' lordship in your life? Why does he call it boasting and bragging when you say *"I'm going to do this and that..."*? (see 1 Corinthians 10:1-6). Is your manner of speaking tainted with arrogance? Are you full of yourself when you give advice or speak to someone? Maybe you need to be listening more and speaking less (James 1:19). "Lord willing" should not become a cliché in your vocabulary, but a testimony of your faith. Your convictions will be exposed by your actions. Continue memorizing and meditating on 2 Corinthians 5:9.

Friday

Read 1 Thessalonians 4:1-5. According to verse 3, what is God's will for you? What is sanctification? What gives you the most pleasure about your life? When our life is driven by our desires and lusts are we in relationship with God? We must learn to control our desires and focus them into a life that is dedicated to pleasing God. Read Galatians 1:10. Who are you currently trying to please the most? If you are trying to please other people can you be a servant of God. Make a list today of three areas you can please God better in, and continue to always ask yourself, "Does this please God?" Continue memorizing and meditating on 2 Corinthians 5:9.

Spend the weekend reviewing what you learned this week.

WEEK 35: *Building Up Others*
(I) Always need spiritual encouragement to endure.
(Therefore, I) Attend regular church meetings.

Monday

Life is a battlefield and it is so easy to feel tired and beat up in your fight against the world. God knows this and that's why he's given us his church as a constant source of encouragement, refreshment, accountability, strength, and support. Read Ephesians 4:11-16. In verse 11, why are your older brothers and sisters put in these positions? What must we be united in? In verse 15 how should we always talk to one another? What is the purpose of being together as a body? Can the body be completely built up if you are not doing your part? Do you see your value to the body of Christ? Or do you think you won't really be missed if you aren't at church? Write Proverbs 11:25 down on an index card and spend this week memorizing and meditating on it throughout the day. Throughout the week, call, email, text or write to different brothers and sisters to refresh them with encouraging words.

Tuesday

Read Ephesians 4:22-32. What are you taught to put off in Christ? What must be made new? When you get together with the church what is your attitude usually like? Do you have an attitude as described in verses 26-27? In verse 29, what should not come out of your mouth? What should only come out? The purpose behind everything we say should be to build others up. When you are around other Christians do they usually feel built up by you or torn down by your attitude or indifference? If you don't go to church meetings can God even use you at all? So how important is it for you to be at all the church meetings? Continue memorizing and meditating on Proverbs 11:25. Who have you called or contacted today?

Wednesday

Remember Ephesians 4:29-32? In verse 30 who will you grieve if you cannot keep your tongue under control? Would you like to be attached to someone who continually grieves you? Verse 31 contains a list of things that grieve the Spirit and your brothers, while verse 32 has a list of things that encourage and edify all. It takes wisdom to know how to build others up. Read James 3:7-18. Do you know the difference between the two kinds of wisdom? What characteristics does heavenly wisdom have? This is the wisdom that builds others up. Continue memorizing and meditating on Proverbs 11:25. Encourage someone today.

Thursday

Read the following analogy the Hebrew writer has given in Hebrews 6:7-8. Who is the land? What is the rain? Who are *"those for whom it is farmed"*? What does it mean by thorns and thistles? As you can see, resistance to the molding hand of God will make you useless in the kingdom. You don't want to be useless. God wants you in the kingdom so you can be useful in his hands. Read 2 Timothy 2:15-16. List the characteristics of an approved workperson. What does such a person avoid? Ungodly talk and godless chatter do not build up the kingdom, but rather they are the type of things that tear it down. Continue memorizing and meditating on Proverbs 11:25. Who have you called or contacted today?

Friday

Read Ephesians 5:1-4 and then Ephesians 5:19-21. The key to building up the church is by being an imitator of who (v. 1)? What type of life will that lead you to live? It always comes back to the heart. Do you have a genuine heart of love for God's people? If not, ask God to help form that in you. In verse 29, what are some of the ways we can live a life of love with our brothers and sisters in Christ? Commit yourself to building up others through spiritual songs, sharing scripture and having a constant attitude of thankfulness and appreciation. Continue memorizing and meditating on Proverbs 11:25. Who have you called or emailed anyone today?

Spend the weekend reviewing what you learned this week.

WEEK 36: *Appreciating Our Differences*
(I) Always need spiritual encouragement to endure.
(Therefore, I) Attend regular church meetings.

Monday

If we examine God's creation we see that God enjoyed making everything unique with different and useful purposes. Read Matthew 13:47-52. What is the kingdom of God compared to? How does this apply to us? Think about how different we all are even in the church! Are our differences usually easy or difficult to deal with? It's usually harder to get along with people that are different from you. Write Ephesians 4:2-3 down on an index card and spend this week memorizing and meditating on it throughout the day.

Tuesday

With yesterday's lesson in mind, read Acts 10 and 11. What was the Lord revealing to Peter? Does it surprise you that Peter and the other disciples had to be taught this even though the Lord's church had been in existence for some time? What did Peter realize through his experience with the Lord (see 10:34)? How about you? Do you show favoritism? Are you more likely to share the gospel with certain people than others? Do you pass up opportunities that the Lord provides for you because you are uncomfortable with some people? Remember that the kingdom is made up of all nations. Especially in the body of Christ we must learn to understand and value our differences. Continue memorizing and meditating on Ephesians 4:2-3.

Wednesday

Read Ephesians 4:16. Does every member of the body have the same function? Can the body be built up completely if some members don't do their part? Are there some members that you value less? Are helpers less important than leaders? Are servants more important than encouragers? Read James 2:1-13. Isn't it awesome how God worked in their lives shaping and molding them? What did James learn about favoritism? Remember that mercy triumphs over judgment. If you have been showing favoritism and judging someone in an ungodly way, now is the time to turn it around. Show the mercy that God has shown you to someone else today. Continue memorizing and meditating on Ephesians 4:2-3.

Thursday

Read Romans 12 with the previous lessons in mind. How should we think of ourselves? Why? What is the danger if we ignore this teaching? What are some of the gifts that God has given to us? What specific gifts has the Lord given to you? How are you using your gifts? Are any of these gifts more important than others? As you realize that the Lord has blessed each of us with particular gifts does it help you to understand why we should honor one another? *How?* Think of a brother or sister who you have not had enough contact with recently. What gift or gifts has the Lord blessed them with? Call them or visit and let them know how encouraged you are about the way the Lord has blessed them and is using them to do his will. Continue memorizing and meditating on Ephesians 4:2-3.

Friday

Read 1 Corinthians 1:26-31. Notice how Paul reminds the Corinthians of who they were when they were called? This is sober reflection of who we are. How can we boast? In whom should we boast? Read chapter 12:12-26 next and see how each of us fits into God's plan. No one is more valuable or more important than anyone else. Truly allow God to cause you to see this clearly because we know this is not true in the world. That is why Paul says what he says in his second letter to the Corinthians. Read 2 Corinthians 5:16-21. How have you been viewing one another? From a worldly or a godly point of view? What do you need to remember in order to have a clear focus? Remember to also view yourself as the new creation that you are in Christ Jesus. Continue memorizing and meditating on Ephesians 4:2-3.

Spend the weekend reviewing what you learned this week.

WEEK 37: Living Faith
(I) Let God's Word Guide my Life.
(Therefore, I) Biblically Memorize and Meditate.

Monday

Read James 2:20-26. We discussed this verse in-depth a few weeks ago. We are revisiting it because one of the hardest things to do in our Christian walk is to live a balanced life. Balancing faith and works is a tough thing to do. The Bible teaches us that we are not saved by works, but by faith (Ephesians 2:8-9). At the same time, the Bible teaches us that faith without works is dead. This week we will be examining passages that will teach us about striking the spiritual balance in our lives that will lead us to growth in Jesus Christ. Read Ecclesiastes 7:15-18. What extremes do you believe Solomon is talking about? Look specifically at verse 16. How can someone be classified as over-righteous (self-righteous)? How about over-wise? Have you ever been self-righteous? Write James 2:22 down on an index card and spend this week memorizing and meditating on it throughout the day.

Tuesday

Today is all about being inspired by the faith of those who have gone before us. Hebrews chapter 11 is known as the *faith* chapter. It's an amazing list of those whose faith was made complete by what they did. Notice verse 6. What *must* you have in order to please God? Notice that the writer gives us a definition of faith in this verse as well. How does the writer define faith? Keeping that definition in mind, read over chapter 11 in Hebrews and describe how each patriarch *showed* his faith. As you see from these examples, faith is shown by what you do. Think about what great stories of faith you would want written about you. Continue memorizing and meditating on James 2:22. Keep living our the word of God in your life.

Wednesday

Read Ephesians 2:8-10. Have we earned salvation or is it a

gift of God? Can you boast about your own works? Why or why not? Even though we aren't saved by our deeds what have we been created to do? Notice the tension between the two. Is this saving grace conditional upon your obedience to the gospel? Read 2 Kings 5:1-15. Did Naaman have to follow God's instructions to be healed of his leprosy? Was it the works that cleansed him, or was it God's grace? Was the healing power in the water or in God? Is your forgiveness of sins conditional on your obedience of the gospel? As you can see from these scriptures, even though we are *not* saved by our *own* deeds (thank God!), we have been created for the purpose of doing good things in the name of God. Continue memorizing and meditating on James 2:22.

Thursday
Read Titus 3:5-7. Is salvation based on righteous works? Why has God saved you? Notice how our redemption comes by the Holy Spirit, whom we received as a *gift*! Notice also, from verse 7, that we have been *justified* (look up this word in a good dictionary) by God's grace, not by anything that we have done or ever will do. By the way, what is the result of this justification? Someone once said the result is "Just as if I'd never sinned." Like Naaman, this justification is conditional on your obedience to the gospel (see Ephesians 2:8-9). Continue memorizing and meditating on James 2:22. Continue obeying God's commands.

Friday
Let's put all of it together: *faith, grace and good works*. Highlight these three words in Ephesians 2:8-10. Read Jude 4. Have you used grace as a license to sin? How does God view this? Read carefully Titus 2:11-14. What has grace taught you? Make a list of the things you need grace to still teach you. Look at verse 13-14. What must you be eager to do? If our lives are well balanced with *grace, faith* and *works*—his appearing should be what we eagerly and hopefully await. Read Romans 6:1-2. Is your life changing? Are you still living your old lifestyle? Continue memorizing and meditating on James 2:22.

Spend the weekend reviewing what you learned this week.

WEEK 38: *Obey God's Commands*
(I) Let God's Word Guide my Life.
(Therefore, I) Biblically Memorize and Meditate.

Monday

Before we can ever obey God's will we must first learn what his will actually is. Read Matthew 7:21-23. What happens when we approach God only with our words "Lord, Lord"? Who are the one's who will enter the kingdom of heaven? Read verses 24-29. What are we like if we hear God's commands but don't put them into practice? What about when we do? Right now, how are you building your life? Read Romans 12:1-2. Are you learning God's good, pleasing and perfect will? Be sure you are practicing the will of God as you learn it. Begin meditating on Luke 6:46.

Tuesday

Read Ephesians 5:22-27. Now look at verse 32. What is the apostle Paul using as a frame of reference when he addresses husband's and wife's attitudes toward each other? From verse 25, how is the husband going to learn to love his wife? How can wives learn to submit to their husbands? As a church, we learn submission to the Lord by recognizing what he does for us. Likewise the husbands have the task of learning the amazing love Jesus has for his church so they can reciprocate this love to their wives. Read verses 25-27 again. Who was the initiator in our relationship with God? Holiness is mentioned at the beginning and at the end. His desire is to make us holy. *How?* Washing and regeneration (Titus 3:5-7). By his Word and his Holy Spirit in us. The point of today's lesson is to not just let God's Word inform you, but transform you. Write Luke 6:46 down on an index card and spend this week memorizing and meditating on it throughout the day.

Wednesday

Read 1 Peter 1:22-23. How are we purified (made holy)?

How can we learn to have sincere love for our brothers and sisters? Notice that loving one another deeply, from the heart includes overlooking fault, sins, and offense. This can only happen when we're imitating God's holiness; when we're obeying the truth. Peter reminds us that this obedience must be the result of our deliverance (verse 23). We have been born again of imperishable seed. *How?* Through the living and enduring word of God. How can his word be living and enduring in you? Read Proverbs 1:7. Continue memorizing and meditating on Luke 6:46.

Thursday

Read 1 Peter 1:14-25 and 1 Peter 2:12-25. In 1:14, what kind of child does God want you to be? In verse 15-16, when you obey God's commands what will you become? In verse 22, when you obey the truth what becomes "sincere" in you? Are you following your emotions that change everyday or the word of God that "stands forever"? Read Ecclesiastes 12:13-14. What is the whole duty of man? Fulfill your life's purpose and duty, and become holy by obeying the commands of God. Think of one of God's commands that you can do better at obeying and ask God to help you fulfill your duty in life to become holy like him. Continue memorizing and meditating on Luke 6:46.

Friday

Read Exodus 20. Here we probably have the most well known commandments in the entire Bible. Go through each command and ask yourself the following question, "In what way am I keeping this command?" When you come to the command regarding the Sabbath, read Colossians 2:14-17. The take away from this week is if you are going to call Jesus Lord you must do what he says. If you aren't really doing what he says then you can't really call him Lord (remember Matthew 7:21). Continue memorizing and meditating on Luke 6:46.

Spend the weekend reviewing what you learned this week.

WEEK 39: A Disciplined Life
(I) Understand my need for godly training.
(Therefore, I) Invite discipling into my life.

Monday

Read 1 Timothy 4:7-11. What should you train yourself to be? Some of us know the discipline it requires to maintain physical fitness, and the importance of that. How much more important and more valuable is becoming and staying *spiritually fit*. Verse 10 holds the key attitude that those who labor and strive for spiritual fitness possess. What and who did Paul put his hope in? What do you put your hope in? It will be shown by what you do. Read 2 Timothy 2:15. Are you willing *"see to it"* that you discipline yourself to this end? Write 1 Timothy 4:7 down on an index card and spend this week memorizing and meditating on it throughout the day.

Tuesday

Read Hebrews 6:11-12. Like trying to stay physically fit, it's easy to get tired and have your drive start to fall asleep. The same happens with our spiritual fitness. To fight this what does the Hebrew writer say that you should do to the very end? What for? What should you not become? How do you *not* become this? As you can see, *discipleship* is key in our spiritual fitness plan. Read Proverbs 24:30-34. What will happen to you if you are lazy? Remember this verse whenever you grow weary. If you are not a punctual person, make an effort to be early. If your quiet times are inconsistent, set a time and place and be diligent to make it happen. Continue memorizing and meditating on 1 Timothy 4:7.

Wednesday

Read 1 Thessalonians 4:11-12. How will you win the respect of outsiders? Have you been a provider or a taker? What does it say about Christ when his followers aren't disciplined? What does your life say about Christ? Read Hebrews 5:11-6:12, you will notice that this whole section deals with some Christians who had become lazy about their spiritual fitness. How do you become spiritually mature and fit according to verse 14? Are you training yourself to be righteous? If you don't keep a scheduled calendar or a to-do list that helps you stay organized then go out today and invest in one. Learn to be responsible with how you manage your time. Continue memorizing and meditating on 1 Timothy 4:7.

Thursday
Discipline protects us from falling into the devil's traps. As the saying goes: *"Idle hands are the devil's workshop..."* The Bible says to stay away from being idle. Carefully read 2 Thessalonians 3:6-15. What is idleness associated with in this verse? What command did Paul give us from the Lord? Read 1 Corinthians 15:58. If you have been idle and burdening to someone, get together with them and pray together to commit to a plan of action that will result in dependence on the Lord and interdependence between each other. Make sure that you are the initiator of this, if indeed you find yourself in this position. Continue memorizing and meditating on 1 Timothy 4:7.

Friday
For many people the idea of discipline is not the most exciting thing to think about. However, it is absolutely necessary to living the life that Christ desires for you. Read Hebrews 12:11-15. Does discipline feel good at the time? What does it produce in the end? Does this happen overnight? Are you willing to be trained by God to be disciplined? Do you want the peace that comes from a disciplined life? Read Proverbs 12:1. What are your strengths and weaknesses in discipline? Spend time with a disciple that is disciplined and learn from their example. Continue memorizing and meditating on 1 Timothy 4:7.

Spend the weekend reviewing what you learned this week.

WEEK 40: Valuing One Another
(I) Understand my need for godly training.
(Therefore, I) Invite discipling into my life.

Monday

Read Mark 12:28-31. God has commanded us to love our neighbors as ourselves. In order for us to fulfill this command we need to learn how to love ourselves. How can we love our neighbor if we cannot love ourselves? In what way can we love ourselves so that it pleases the Lord? In John 12:20-26 Jesus teaches us that we must hate our lives in this world to follow him. Love your life in Christ, but hate your life that's corrupted by the world. So how should you love your life in Christ? Read 1 Peter 2:9-ff. How does God describe you in verses 9-10? How did he show you how valuable you are to him (read verses 24-ff)? Read Romans 8:15-17. As adopted children of God we cry out "Abba" (Daddy), Father. The Lord has adopted each of us to be his own and he is our Daddy, our Father. Esteem (value) yourself, because God loves you. With that said, stay humble and write Philippians 2:3-4 down on an index card and spend this week memorizing and meditating on it throughout the day.

Tuesday

Today I want you to take the love you have for yourself and focus it on how you can love others better. Read Colossians 3:12-14. How are we addressed by God? If you were to look at this as a recipe for perfect unity—what would the essential ingredients be? What is the main ingredient? Now read the chapter from beginning to end. The keys to great relationships are here. As you read, notice your need to remember who you were—who you are now in the Lord—and how we are to be different. If we have the ingredients as described in verses 12-14 then we can successfully fulfill verse 18-ff. Continue memorizing and meditating on Philippians 2:3-4.

Wednesday

Read Ephesians 4:29-32. Only wholesome words should

come out of our mouths. Do you see the ingredients for unity (great relationships) in these verses? Very similar to what we read in Colossians, isn't it? Notice that we need to know what each others needs are in order to build one another up. This is absolutely key to having great relationships. The opportunity for true loving relationships has been given to each of us. Combine your words with action—read John 13:1-17 and seek to imitate the Lord's love today. Look at verse 34 as well and notice the results of our love for one another. It is the most powerful testimony to the world that we are truly Jesus' disciples. Continue memorizing and meditating on Philippians 2:3-4.

Thursday

Read Proverbs 18:19-21. When you value something how do you treat it? If you truly value your brothers in sisters in Christ how should you treat them? If you de-value them and therefore don't pay close attention to your words what can your word do to others? What does verse 21 say about the power of the tongue? Read Colossians 3:18-21 again. If you have cut anyone with your words call them today and ask for their forgiveness. With repentance comes times of refreshing from the Lord (Acts 3:19-20). Continue memorizing and meditating on Philippians 2:3-4.

Friday

In Philippians 2, the Lord teaches us that we must honor (value, esteem) one another above ourselves. His example to us is exactly that—he honors us above himself and that is how he shows he loves us. The key though is humility. Read Ephesians 4:1-16. Humility is absolutely necessary for unity and love. Without humility we will not attain maturity in Christ nor will we have the love we all need so much. Pursue love (1 Timothy 6:11-16), strive for it in all your relationships because God is love (1 John 4:16). Continue memorizing and meditating on Philippians 2:3-4.

Spend the weekend reviewing what you learned this week.

WEEK 41: A Ministry of Reconciliation
(I) Enjoy bringing souls to Christ.
(Therefore, I) Tell others the good news.

Monday

We've already learned about reconciling the lost to God, but reconciliation (healing what's broken) must also happen inside the church (2 Corinthians 5:20). This week we are going to learn about how true love heals and transforms all relationships. Read Romans 12. This chapter paints an amazing picture of what we are to become if we desire to be used by God in a ministry of reconciliation (especially vv. 9-21). Write each of the qualities of love you see in these verses on paper—this will be our vision list. Before each quality write down " Love is..." and then write the quality in present tense. For example from 9 you can write: "Love is sincere. Love hates what is evil. Love clings to what is good." When you are done go through each one and ask God to help you live out each of these qualities in your life. The more your love grows for others the more effective you'll be in your ministry of reconciliation. Write 2 Corinthians 5:20 down on an index card and spend this week memorizing and meditating on it throughout the day.

Tuesday

Read 1 Corinthians 13:1-8. Compare the list you made yesterday to this passage. As you read these verses put Jesus' name in place of the word love. He fulfills each quality perfectly because he is love. Now do the same with your own name. Repeat this exercise frequently as a spiritual workout. Allow yourself to be transformed by the power of God and become more like him as you practice and become more loving. Continue memorizing and meditating on 2 Corinthians 5:20.

Wednesday

The Lord clearly teaches us what love is and that it is the fulfillment of all that God has commanded us (see Romans 13). He also teaches us how we can become stumbling blocks to one another when we don't love. Today we will read Romans 14. Read carefully and ask yourself if you have been or are a stumbling block to those you have been called to love. If we act in a way which is destructive to a brother or sister are we acting in love (see verse 15)? According to this verse, is it possible to destroy a brother or sister (for whom Christ died) through our own discouraging, and unloving behavior? What is the kingdom of God all about in verses 17-18? In 19-21 what is required for great loving relationships (unity)? Pray again through the vision list you wrote on Monday. Continue memorizing and meditating on 2 Corinthians 5:20.

Thursday

Sometimes in our relationships instead of reconciling them we can break them further. Reread Ephesians 4:31-32. In verse 31 we see the qualities which break, hurt, offend and destroy relationships. What does 32 teach? What is the motivation for us? From chapter 5:1-2 what is our calling? We are to live lives of love as Jesus did. Read 1 John 2:6 and 2 John 6. Dwell on these and pray to God to help you become more like Jesus in his love for other people. Continue memorizing and meditating on 2 Corinthians 5:20.

Friday

Read Philippians 2:1-21. The calling of the Lord's church is to love and to be unified in spirit and purpose. In verses 3-4, where should we put our interests? In verse 21, where do our interests naturally go? It's so easy to see human selfishness in the relationships of the world. Great relationships are found where people are constantly putting each other first. When this happens verses 12-18 show us that we will become so different that we will shine like stars in the universe. Remember that the more loving you become the more your light will shine and the more souls you will be reconciled to God. Continue memorizing and meditating on 2 Corinthians 5:20.

Spend the weekend reviewing what you learned this week.

WEEK 42: *You are the Salt of the Earth*
(I) Enjoy bringing souls to Christ.
(Therefore, I) Tell others the good news.

Monday

Jesus compares us to two things that are very influential: light and salt. Whatever these two things touch cannot ignore their presence. You can always count on them too; they will never fail to do what they're supposed to do, unless of course, they are not the real thing. This week you will learn how to be the salt Jesus says you are. Read Matthew 5:13. What are some characteristics of salt? What is salt good for? How is it influential? When you are around people in the world do they influence you more or do you influence them more (read 1 Corinthians 15:33). Make a list of ways you let others influence you more and ask God to help you reverse that and make you the salt of the earth. Write Matthew 5:13 down on an index card and spend this week memorizing and meditating on it throughout the day.

Tuesday

Read Romans 12:1-2. Salt is a preservative. It prevents corruption from taking place. In what ways are you staying uncorrupted by the world? Are you to conform to (be like) the world in what you do? How are you to transform? Just like salt transforms everything that it touches, so are you to transform (influence) yourself and others. What is the purpose of transformation? Can this purpose be accomplished without transformation? Read 2 Peter 1:4. Notice how you escape corruption by partaking of God's divine nature. Be careful then you allow things to impact your nature like what you read, what you watch on television, the music you listen to, the movies you see. Read James 1:27. Are you striving to keep yourself from being corrupted by the world? Continue memorizing and meditating on Matthew 5:13.

Wednesday

Since salt prevents corruption from taking place, it has a purifying effect. Read 2 Kings 2:20-21. What effect did the salt have on the water? What symbolism did the salt have in this miracle that the Lord did through Elisha? *Think about the purifying effect of God's command, its influence and its permanence.* In the same way the Lord purifies you. Read Titus 2:14. How are God's people purified in this verse? What the salt did to Elisha's water God does to you: purifies and makes you fruitful; zealous for good deeds. How is zeal for good deeds like salt? Read 2 Corinthians 7:1. Make a list of ways you can be more impactful. Continue memorizing and meditating on Matthew 5:13.

Thursday

Being salt not only involves keeping yourself pure from the corruption of the world but also keeping God's doctrine pure in your heart, mind and soul. Read 2 Timothy 2:15. Being salty means being able to use God's Word adequately. You want to be salty enough so that people see something different in you. Think of potato chips. You can't just have one. Read 2 Timothy 2:2. Being salty means being reliable in the Word; ably qualified to teach others God's Word, not your own word. Salt preserves. That means it keeps things pure by making sure nothing gets into it and corrupts it. Read 1 Timothy 4:16. When you share your faith with others do they see that you practice what you preach? Continue memorizing and meditating on Matthew 5:13.

Friday

Salt's influence is very powerful; just like light's influence on darkness. No matter how little there is of it in something, its presence is felt and noted. Its effects are not overcome or diminished even though there might only be a small quantity. Read Mark 9:50. Is it possible for salt to loose its saltiness? Can you loose your focus to impact others? Read Colossians 4:6. Knowing how to speak to someone involves being able and willing to preserve peace and grace. Is your speech salty or bitter? Does your lifestyle reflect the saltiness Jesus speaks of, or does it reflect the corruption of the world? Continue memorizing and meditating on Matthew 5:13.

Spend the weekend reviewing what you learned this week.

WEEK 43: *The Most Excellent Way*
(I) Sincerely care about the needs of others.
(Therefore, I) Serve others with my S.H.A.P.E.

Monday

Read Matthew 22:34-40 and Mark 12:28-34. Jesus quotes Deuteronomy 6:5 and Leviticus 19:18, and he is the first to combine these two texts to summarize the law into the two greatest commandments. He also mentions something we are to use to fully love the Lord that the text in Deuteronomy 6 does not mention. What is it? What does this tell you about how to love the Lord? Read Galatians 5:13-15 today. Do something for your neighbor to show God's love. Do something that you would like done to you today. Write Mark 12:31 down on an index card and spend this week memorizing and meditating on it throughout the day.

Tuesday

Read Deuteronomy 6. Since the very beginning of the Bible God wanted his people's love to be behind everything they did. In 6:6-9, did God want our love to be a private affair or a family affair? What did the Lord tell them to teach their children in verses 20-25? How does this apply to you and your need to share the gospel? Remember 2 Corinthians 5:14-15? Our love for God is still the motivating force behind everything we do. Continue memorizing and meditating on Mark 12:31.

Wednesday

Read Deuteronomy 8-10 today. As you read the text, notice what the Lord stresses to his children. In verses 1 through 5, why was it important for God's children to be tested the way they were? Take note of how God tells the Israelites to remember their blessings. What will happen to them if they forget the Lord? Have you noticed as you read these chapters how many times the Lord tells them to remember him? In chapter 9, why was God going to give the Israelites this great promised land? What kind of attitude was the Lord warning them about in verse 4? In Deuteronomy 10:12-ff, can you see the two greatest commandments? Who are we to love above all else? How are we to treat others around us? *Why?* Continue memorizing and meditating on Mark 12:31.

Thursday
    Read Deuteronomy 11. What is God calling his children to do? Notice how the elements of loving, fearing and obeying God are repeated again and again? God says to his people in verse 26, *"see I am setting before you today a blessing and a curse..."* What is the blessing and the curse God is talking about? Pray to the Lord to constantly open your eyes to see his blessings in your life. Be prepared to see wonderful things that you may not have seen before and be prepared as God reminds you of his love for you. Your love for God will stay fresh as long as you continually remember his love for you and the blessings he gives. Continue memorizing and meditating on Mark 12:31.

Friday
    Read Revelation 2:1-7. What happens to a church that forgets it's first love? The church at Ephesus had some great qualities. What were they? What happened to them? What was the Spirit convicting them of? What was going to be their outcome if they did not repent? What would be their blessing if they listened and what would be their curse if they did not? Now read Ephesians 3:14-20. Knowing what the Ephesians were being convicted of in Revelation 2, you can appreciate why Paul prayed for them the way he did. Look at Revelation 2:17-19 in particular. What did they need to grow in their understanding of? Pray as Paul did: that we, as a church, will grow continuously in our understanding and appreciation of God's awesome love for each and every one of us. It's only when we grasp God's love for us that we will truly be about to love others they way he wants us to. Make a list of the ways God has shown his love for you. Continue memorizing and meditating on Mark 12:31.

Spend the weekend reviewing what you learned this week.

WEEK 44: *Use Your Gifts to Serve Others*
(I) Sincerely care about the needs of others.
(Therefore, I) Serve others with my S.H.A.P.E.

Monday

One of the greatest struggles believers have is acknowledging the gifts that God has given them. This week we will cover how gifted you really are in Christ and how God expects you to prove faithful with them. Read Luke 12:42-48. What has this manager been put in charge of (v. 42)? Was he faithful with what he was given? Notice that verses 46 and 47 depict the manager that is unfruitful and unproductive (unfaithful). What are some characteristics of this manager? Does he manage God's blessings well? What will be the end for this manager? From verse 47, what does the manager have to know? How are you managing what God has given you? What will God do if you aren't proving faithful with what he's give you (v. 48)? Write Luke 12:48 down on an index card and spend this week memorizing and meditating on it throughout the day.

Tuesday

Read Luke 19:12-27. To each servant the Lord gives one mina, totaling ten. A mina is a measure of Greek money, equivalent to three months salary. What are the servants told to do in verse 13? What was the response of his subjects? Could it be that they didn't want to work hard? Could it be that they didn't want to earn their responsibility? There were at least two servants that didn't respond negatively. Describe what these servants did. What do you think their attitude was? Look at the Master's response. What does he call the servants who earned more from the solitary mina they were given? Notice he describes them as trustworthy. What does he call the servant who just simply returned the mina? What was the attitude of this servant? Who are you most like in this parable? Continue memorizing and meditating on Luke 12:48.

Wednesday

The parable of the talents is found in Matthew 25:14-30. Notice that each slave receives talents according to their abilities, in contrast to the parable of the minas in which each servant receives the same amount. This could be that the mina stands for the life which God gives each of us to live, where the talents represent the gifts and abilities that God gives each of us and makes each of us different. Make a list of the blessings, gifts, and talents that God has given you. Do you realize that depending on how you *manage* these things that God could take them away from you or put you in charge of more things and perhaps bless you with more abilities? Continue memorizing and meditating on Luke 12:48.

Thursday

Read Luke 8:4-15. Four soils are described. One soil proved to be very fruitful. If you were the farmer, would you be pleased with soil that does not produce a crop? Why not? What would you do with the thorns? What kind of soil are you? If you are not deeply rooted in the Word and are worried by the things of the world (not trusting in God) then you are not the good soil. What three things characterize the good soil? The seed on good soil lets the Word mature them so they can produce (v. 15). Continue memorizing and meditating on Luke 12:48.

Friday

Read 2 Chronicles 34 and 35. According to verse 2 in chapter 34, did Josiah seek to follow his own way, or the ways of his father? According to verse three, what caused Josiah to begin reform throughout Judah and Jerusalem? What was Josiah's response when he heard the word of God (v.19)? What was God's response (v.27)? From verses 31-33, would you say that Josiah was a lazy servant of God? What kind of revival happened due to his renewed commitment (35:18)? Did the people miss him when he died (35:24-25)? Do you think he put his talents to work? Continue memorizing and meditating on Luke 12:48.

Spend the weekend reviewing what you learned this week.

Possess these qualities in increasing measure...and you will never fall! 119

WEEKS 45-52: *Psalms and Proverbs*

Over the next 60 days you are going to read two of the most inspiring and practical books in the entire Bible. The book of Psalms, largely written by King David, will show you the heart of God and the heart of one of his greatest servants. The book of Proverbs, written by David's son, King Solomon, will show you the wisdom of God and how it can be applied to your daily life.

6 Quick Tips for Bible Reading

1. Begin by praying for God's help and end your reading by praying the A.C.T.S.

2. Don't worry about understanding and remembering everything you read.

3. At the end of each chapter write in a notebook what stood out to you the most.

4. If you have any questions write them down and ask an older disciple at a later time.

5. Write down how you think today's reading can help you in your new values and habits.

6. Pick one verse each week from your reading to memorize and meditate on.

30 Days in the Psalms

Day	Theme	Passage
1	Blessings	Psalm 67, 72, 128
2	Calling to God	Psalm 4, 5, 22
3	Confidence	Psalm 27, 36, 125
4	Deeds of God	Psalm 9, 18, 118
5	Doubt	Psalm 42, 73, 77
6	Faithfulness of God	Psalm 105,119:137-144
7	Fear	Psalm 37, 49, 91
8	Glory of God	Psalm 19, 24, 29
9	God is a Helper	Psalm 54, 119:169–176

V.A.l.U.E.S. & H.A.B.I.T.S. of spiritual growth

10	Identity	Psalm 8, 139
11	Justice of God	Psalm 7, 26, 82
12	Meditation	Psalm 119:9–16, 41–48
13	Mercy	Psalm 13, 28, 86
14	Music	Psalm 6, 149, 150
15	Nature	Psalm 50, 104, 147, 148
16	Peace	Psalm 23, 119:161–168
17	Power of God	Psalm 68, 93, 135
18	Praise	Psalm, 65, 98, 138
19	Prayer	Psalm 17, 20, 102
20	Protection	Psalm 59, 62, 124
21	Safety in God	Psalm 11, 16, 142, 46
22	Rejoicing	Psalm 30, 47, 97
23	Righteousness	Psalm 1, 15, 112
24	Salvation	Psalm 3, 14, 121
25	Sin and Repentance	Psalm 25, 32, 38, 51
26	Thanksgiving	Psalm 75, 106, 136
27	Trust	Psalm 31, 40, 56
28	Victory	Psalm 21, 76, 144
29	Wisdom	Psalm 90, 107, 111
30	Worship	Psalm 33, 34, 145

30 Days In Proverbs

1	Proverbs 1	15	Proverbs 15
2	Proverbs 2	16	Proverbs 16
3	Proverbs 3	17	Proverbs 17
4	Proverbs 4	18	Proverbs 18
5	Proverbs 5	19	Proverbs 19
6	Proverbs 6	20	Proverbs 20
7	Proverbs 7	21	Proverbs 21
8	Proverbs 8	22	Proverbs 22
9	Proverbs 9	23	Proverbs 23
10	Proverbs 10	24	Proverbs 24
11	Proverbs 11	25	Proverbs 25
12	Proverbs 12	26	Proverbs 26
13	Proverbs 13	27	Proverbs 27
14	Proverbs 14	28	Proverbs 28
		29	Proverbs 29
		30	Proverbs 30-31

Discipleship Guide

A weekly guide for another disciple

to help you make the most of this journey

Aftercare

Although you may be using this "Discipleship Guide" with another brother or sister who just wants to strengthen themselves spiritually, this particular section regarding "Aftercare" is specifically for those working with new disciples in Christ.

A soul was saved! One of God's lost children has come home. Their sins have been washed away in the waters of baptism. Now what? Now the real work begins.

Baptism was the quick and easy part. Whether it took a day, a week, a month or a year to decide to be born again (John 3:5), it's just the beginning. Jesus says, *"He who stands firm until the end will be saved"* (Mark 13:13). In other words, after baptism the real work of helping the new disciple *"finish the race and keep the faith"* (2 Timothy 4:7) begins. If we don't take care of the young disciple and they fall away, 2 Peter 2:20 clearly states that they end up in a worse state than before they made Jesus Lord. Therefore, if we are going to bring people to Christ we must also commit the time, energy, and resources to helping them remain in Christ until they cross the finish line.

The Goal of Aftercare

If Satan attacked Jesus immediately after his baptism (Matthew 4) we know he's going to do the same to the new disciple. This is why the days, weeks, and months following their baptism are an absolutely critical time for them to grow roots in Christ, in prayer, in his Word, and in the church. *Aftercare* is about loving, strengthening and protecting them during this time.

2 Peter 1:8-10 says that, *"if you possess these qualities in increasing measure...you will never fall."* In other words, those

who stay faithful in Christ are those who never stop growing in their walk with Christ. Therefore, the ultimate goal of the *Aftercare* program is, at the end of their first year in Christ, to help the new disciple develop a few of the core biblical principles that are essential for lifelong growth in Christ (V.A.L.U.E.S. & H.A.B.I.T.S.—see Diagram I on page 3). The two acronyms are designed to make those principles easier to remember and to apply. Each acronym represents: 1) What you do (habits), and 2) why you do it (values). For example, many Christians break the habit of "A-ttending regular church meetings" because they lose the value that they "A-lways need encouragement to endure."

What does Aftercare require of me?

So what will *Aftercare* require of you? Jesus says that the greatest command is to love God will all of our heart, soul, mind and strength (Mark 12:30), and that we should also love one another with a similar kind of love. In other words, you must be willing to give the new disciple your heart, soul, mind, and strength as well. We all tend to be stronger in one or two of these areas, but for their sake we must strive to invest all four!

Heart: Give them your heart. Develop a personal relationship that shows you care and know them.

Soul: Make the long-term commitment to their growth and the eternal destination of their soul.

Mind: Share with them what you know about the word of God and how to apply it to everyday life.

Strength: It takes real effort to build a friendship and to train another disciple. Make every effort.

As the new disciple goes through the year-long quiet time series this companion discipleship guide follows their weekly studies so that each week you can meet, follow up, and build upon what they are learning. It's especially important during their first year in Christ when you are intentionally building up their faith and not just making up lessons on the fly that don't connect with what they are learning.

The Meeting Structure

Jesus says, *"teach them to obey everything I have com-manded you,"* but then he leaves it up to us to decide how ex-actly to teach them. For example, should you meet one-on-one like Jesus did with Peter (John 21), or meet in a small group like Jesus did with Peter, James and John (Matthew 17), or slightly larger like he did with the twelve? Should you meet once a day, once a week, once every two weeks, etc? How long should you meet for…one hour, two, three? The Bible doesn't say. So here are just a few guidelines that I personally find helpful.

1) **Establish a consistent discipleship time**
    a. During their first year in Christ I personally recommend trying to meet weekly. As they mature and need less time together you can eventually adjust the schedule.
    b. Set aside 1½ to 2 hours to meet. Less than this tends to feel rushed and limits the depth of your discussion. Over 2 hours is too long for most people (Ecclesiastes 6:11).

2) **Establish "non-formal" fellowship**
    a. Some of us are better relationally than others. If that's not a strength of yours always remember that this isn't a busi-ness meeting, but rather disciples spending time together trying to love one another and help each other grow.

3) **Be disciplined about covering the weekly material.**
    a. Some of us are better at structure than others. If that's not a strength of yours always remember that besides be-ing friends you also want to *"teach them to obey all that Christ has commanded."* This takes being prepared and largely sticking to the weekly review of their quiet times.

3) **Model what you want from them.**
    a. If you want them to be open about their struggles you must model this by being open about your own.

---

b. If you want them to seek advice about life matters than humble yourself and seek their advice. They'll do what you do before they do what you say.

Aftercare In The Family Group

Maturing a new disciple is a "family affair" and will require the help of everyone in your family or small group. Some will be more involved than others, but everyone must understand that God expects them to not only be a part of evangelism, but also a part of maturing the new convert. Obviously everyone does not play the same role. Some will be the primary discipler for the new convert while others will help in various supporting roles ranging from building a friendship, praying for them, giving advice, and helping support the overall maturing process.

The following are a few suggestions for those not directly responsible for the new Christian on how they can build up the new member. It is only a partial list and will require you to modify the approach to fit the new convert and the family group.

Visit Them: In the first three months especially, make time to just get together and get to know one another.

Call Them: Weekly phone calls do not replace visiting them, but it's great to just check in as a friend.

Serve Them: If you don't have time to get together nothing is better than giving some cookies or brownies to show them that you care and were thinking about them.

Send Cards: Send a card to your new brother/sister at least once a month to share how proud you are of them.

Sit Together: Sit with them during worship services.

Pray with and for them: Pray with them at every turn especially during any visit for any reason. Model God's call for us to pray and talk to him without ceasing. Also, pray for them even when they aren't around.

I pray God will use you to love and mature many disciples!

V.A.L.U.E.S & H.A.B.I.T.S. (Diagram I)

(I)   (Therefore, I)

V-alue my relationship w/ God, above all. • **H**-ave a daily Quiet Time.

The greatest command in the bible is to love God (Mark 12:30) above all (Matt 10:37). That love is built by listening to Him (2 Timothy 3:16), and speaking to Him (1 Thessalonians 5:17) everyday.

A-lways need encouragement to endure. • **A**-ttend church services.

We are saved if we stay faithful till the end (Mark 13:13). That's why we must meet regularly to encourage one another (Hebrews 10:25) to stay encouraged and faithful (Hebrews 3:13).

L-et God's Word guide my life. • **B**-iblically memorize and meditate.

Our ways lead to death (Proverbs 16:25), but God's ways lead to life. We change our ways by renewing our minds (Romans 12:2) and replacing our thoughts with God's thoughts (Psalms 119:11, 97-99).

U-nderstand my need for godly training. • **I**-nvite discipling in my life.

We all need to continually be taught to obey God's commands (Matthew 28:20). This happens by "one another" relationships (Hebrews 3:23, 10:23) and learning from more mature disciples (Titus 2:3-7).

E-njoy bringing souls to Christ. • **T**-ell others the Good News.

When you love someone you want to give them what they want, and God wants all men to be saved (1 Timothy 2:4). That is the great commission God has given you (Matthew 28:19-20).

S-incerely meet the needs of others. • **S**-erve others with my S.H.A.P.E.

Becoming more like Christ means that we genuinely care about the needs of others (Philippians 2:3-4, 20). God has given you spiritual gifts (Romans 12:6-8) to serve and meet those needs (Galatians 6:10).

- Open up with a word of prayer.
- How are you doing? How was your first week in Christ?
- How's life? Work? Family?
- Share about your life. Model openness and seek their input.
- How were your Q.T.'s? Prayer life? Consistency is key.
- Let's review this week's quiet times together.

Review Day 1: 40 Days In The Desert

Q: What was the main point of that lesson (reread if needed)?
- Be on alert for Satan's schemes (Matt. 3:16, Eph. 6:10-11)

Q: How has Satan been attacking you this week?

Review Day 2: Growing Roots

Q: What was the main point of that lesson?
- Grow roots or Satan will pull you away (Luke 8:13).

Q: Do you remember the 2 acronyms that the book is based on?
Q: Did you write them a note card like it suggested?

Q: What stood out to you from days 3-7?
Q: Do you remember the first *Value and Habit*? (page 127).
Q: Do you remember the verse that goes with each? (page 127).

Mark 12:28-31 (memory verse #1)
1. What is the most important command or value in the Bible?
2. Why do you think it is more important than anything else?
3. Is your relationship with God first? (Matthew 10:37-39).

James 4:8 (memory verse #2)
1. If you draw closer to God what will he do in return?
2. How do you think you can get closer to God?

Like a marriage you build a relationship with God by talking with him everyday. Listen to him through his Word and speak to him in prayer. *(Close in prayer. Set up another time this week to hang out and have fun.)*

Week Two: *Their Relationship with the Church*

- Open up with a word of prayer.
- How are you doing? Life? Work? Family?
- Share about your life. Model openness and seek their input.
- How were your Q.T.'s? Prayer life? Consistency is key.

Review Day 9: Family of God
Q: What was the main point of that lesson (reread if needed)?
- Those born again are "blood" family (Mark 3:31-35).
Q: Do you see God's church as your spiritual family?

Review Day 10: Unity In Christ
Q: What is unity and why is it so important (Palms 133:1-3)?

Review Day 11: Worship in Spirit and Truth
Let's turn to John 4:22-24 and spend a little extra time here.
1. Does it matter where you go to worship God?
2. What two things do you want to be sure you worship in?
3. What do you think it means to worship in spirit and truth?
4. Should you want to worship with a group that teaches an unbiblical way of being saved?
5. If they aren't really saved do they have the Holy Spirit?
6. If so, is attending there worshipping in spirit and in truth?
7. What's good to do before visiting a church? (Acts 17:11).

Day 12-14 : Pressure and Discouragements
Q: How's your family doing with your decision? If not good:
- How did Jesus handle his family when they weren't supportive (Mark 3:20-21, John 7:1-9). (Encourage them to stay strong.)
Q: Do you remember the second *Value and Habit*? (page 127).
Q: Do you remember the verse that goes with each? (page 127).

Remember how important the church is to helping you fight the deceitfulness of sin (Hebrews 3:12-14). We need daily encouragement. *(Close in a prayer. Set up another time this week if you can to just hang out and have fun.)*

Week Three: *Their Relationship with the Word*

- Open up with a word of prayer.
- How are you doing? How's life? Work? Family?
- Share about your life. Model openness and seek their input.
- How were your Q.T.'s? Prayer life? Consistency is key.
- Let's review this week's quiet times together.

Review Day 15: God's Word Guides My Life
Q: What was the main point of that lesson (reread if needed)?
- God's Word is my new value system (2 Timothy 3:16-17).

Q: What was your old standard for making decisions?
Q: How much did your friends influence you (1 Cor. 15:33)?

Review Day 16: Obey God
Q: What was the main point of that lesson?
- The mark of a true disciple is obedience to God (John 8:31).

Review Day 17: Wrestling with Doubts
Q: Is there any Bible teachings that you still have doubts about?
- If you don't have an answer tell them you'll get back to them.

Day 18: Disputable Matters
Q: What are some disputable matters among Christians today?
- Based on Romans 14:1-8, apart from the clear doctrinal truths the Bible teaches, what should your attitude be toward those who see these things differently than you?

Q: Do you remember the third *Value and Habit*? (page 127).
Q: Do you remember the verse that goes with each? (page 127).

1 John 5:3
1. How is real love for God expressed? Are you showing it?

(Close in a prayer. Set up another time this week if you can to just hang out and have fun.)

Week Four: *Their Relationship with a Discipleship Partner*

- Open up with a word of prayer.
- How are you doing? How's life? Work? Family?
- Share about your life. Model openness and seek their input.
- How were your Q.T.'s? Prayer life? Consistency is key.
- Let's review this week's quiet times together.

Review Day 20: I Will Learn from Others
Q: What was the main point of this lesson?
- That older disciples are to teach younger disciples to obey everything Christ has commanded.

Review Day 21: Being Open and Honest
Start by reading John 15:15.
Q: What did Jesus share with his disciples?
Q: Are you this kind of a friend to other disciples?
Q: Do you share your life with friends in the church?

Review Day 22: Confessing Sin
(Read Proverbs 28:13; James 5:16)
Q: Can we conceal our sins from God?
Q: What effect will concealed sin have in our life?
Q: Who do we need to confess our sins to besides God?
Q: Are there any sins you have been afraid to confess?

Review Day 23: I'll Take Correction
Q: What does correction bring? (Proverbs 15:31-32)
Q: Do you remember the fourth *Value and Habit*? (page 127).
Q: Do you remember the verse that goes with each? (page 127).

(Close in a prayer. Set up another time this week if you can to just hang out and have fun.)

- Open up with a word of prayer.
- How are you doing? How's life? Work? Family?
- Share about your life. Model openness and seek their input.
- How were your Q.T.'s? Prayer life? Consistency is key.
- Let's review this week's quiet times together.

Review Day 26: I Will Go and Make Disciples

Q: What is the great commission (Matthew 28:19-20)?
- Preach the gospel…and go make disciples!
- Grow in your love for the lost. Ask God to help you to love souls the way He does, and to use you to bring others to him.

Review Day 27: Too Good to Keep

Q: What was the main point of this lesson?
- Don't be discouraged by people's poor reaction to the gospel.
- If someone is open, contact them and set up a Bible study.

Review Day 28: I Am Saved to Save

Q: How did Paul use his freedom in Christ (1 Cor. 9:19-27)?
Q: Are you using yours to impact others for Jesus Christ?
Q: Did you make a list of who you want to see come to Christ? (If so, great. If not make a quick list and pray over it together!)
Q: How do you think you could lead these people to Christ?

Review Day 30: Shining Like Stars

Q: How can you hold out the word of life (Philippians 2:14-16)?
Q: How is your example to others around you?
Q: Do you remember the fifth *Value and Habit*? (page 127).
Q: Do you remember the verse that goes with each? (page 127).

(Close in a prayer. Set up another time this week if you can to just hang out and have fun.)

- Open up with a word of prayer.
- How are you doing? How's life? Work? Family?
- Share about your life. Model openness and seek their input.
- How were your Q.T.'s? Prayer life? Consistency is key.
- Let's review this week's quiet times together.

Review Day 36: I Am Saved to Serve

Q: When we serve those who are hurting in the kingdom, who are we really serving (Matthew 25:31-46)?—Jesus!

Q: Which of the six things listed in verses 35-36 have you done recently?

Review Days 33-39: Discover your S.H.A.P.E.

If you have not done so already, go to pages 52-64 and spend the next several days discovering your own **S.H.A.P.E.**

The key to this acronym is: First, to help them understand that they have a place in the church, and that they do have a lot to offer. Second, great relationships are built on understanding and valuing our differences. Really get to know them by spending quality time sharing each of your SHAPE's.

Q: Do you remember the sixth *Value and Habit?* (page 127).

Q: Do you remember the verse that goes with each? (page 127).

Congratulations, you have survived "40 Days In The Desert." Hopefully, in the past 40 days you have begun to develop the critical V.A.L.U.E.S. and H.A.B.I.T.S. of a growing disciple! As you continue your spiritual journey everything you learn with build upon these critical principles. It's important to always continue growing because the moment you stop growing spiritually you start dying spiritually. Keep fighting the good fight and finish the race of faith!

(Close in a prayer.)

Week 7: *Communicating with God—Listen*
(I) Value my relationship with God, above all.
(Therefore, I) Have a Daily Quiet Time.

- Open up with a word of prayer.
- How are you doing? How's life?
- Share about your life. Model openness and seek their input.
- How were your quiet times? Prayer life? Consistency is key.
- Let's review this week's quiet times together.

Can you quote the memory verse? Matthew 4:4.
As you review the quiet times from the past week:
1. Reread the main scripture for each day of the week together.
2. How did this verse relate to the theme of the week?
3. How did you feel this verse applied to you personally?

> **Review Monday:** Read 2 Timothy 3:16.
> **Review Tuesday:** Read Psalm 119:97-104.
> **Review Wednesday:** Read Romans 12:1-2.
> **Review Thursday:** Read James 1:22-25.
> **Review Friday:** Read James 1:22-25.

Conclusion:

1 Corinthians 1:9 says that God has called us into fellowship with Jesus Christ. Christianity is all about a relationship with God. A real relationship involves listening and speaking to one another. Everyday you should draw close to God (James 4:8) and listen to him as he tries to show you his heart and will through his Word. Finally, being in the Word is also our way of finding out what pleases our Lord and Savior (Ephesians 5:9).

Application:

1. Hear are some practical suggestions:
2. Have a set time and place to study your Bible daily.
3. Keep a note book to write down the convicting points or questions from your quiet time.

Week 8: Communicating with God—Speak
(I) Value my relationship with God, above all.
(Therefore, I) Have a Daily Quiet Time.

- Open up with a word of prayer.
- How are you doing? How's life?
- Share about your life. Model openness and seek their input.
- How were your quiet times? Prayer life? Consistency is key.
- Let's review this week's quiet times together.

Can you quote the memory verse? Romans 8:15.
As you review the quiet times from the past week:
1. Reread the main scripture for each day of the week.
2. How did this verse relate to the theme of the week?
3. How did you feel this verse applied to you personally?

Review Monday: Read Luke 11:1-4.
Review Tuesday: Read Matthew 6:6-15.
Review Wednesday: Read Ephesians 3:14-15.
Review Thursday: Read Ephesians 6:18.
Review Friday: Read Proverbs 3:5.

Conclusion:
Throughout the Bible God asks his children to be devoted to talking to him (prayer). God wants to hear from you, connect with you and walk with you everyday of your life. They don't have to be long or complicated. Just talk to God like a friend.

Application:
Hear are some practical suggestions:

1. Set a regular time to pray every day.

2. Here is a great acronym to help you pray. **A-C-T-S:**
Adoration	**1 Chronicles 29:10-13**
Confession	**Proverbs 28:13**
Thanksgiving	**Philippians 4:6**
Supplication	**John 14:13**

Week 9: Relationships in Christ
(I) Always need spiritual encouragement to endure.
(Therefore, I) Attend regular church meetings.

- Open up with a word of prayer.
- How are you doing? How's life?
- Share about your life. Model openness and seek their input.
- How were your Q.T.'s? Prayer life? Consistency is key.
- Let's review this week's quiet times together.

Can you quote the memory verse? Hebrews 10:24-25.
As you review the quiet times from the past week:
1. Reread the main scripture for each day of the week.
2. How did this verse relate to the theme of the week?
3. How did you feel this verse applied to you personally?

Review Monday: Read John 13:34-35.
Review Tuesday: Read Philippians 2:5-7.
Review Wednesday: Read Acts 2:42-47.
Review Thursday: Read Hebrews 3:12-13.
Review Friday: Read 1 Thessalonians 5:11-13.

Conclusion:

The church family for most of us is radically different than our physical family. Instead of having ourselves as our focus, we must consider others as better than ourselves (Philippians 2:3). God gave us the church because we need each others support if we are ever going to finish the race and keep the faith!

Application:

Here are some practical suggestions:

1. Introduce yourself to someone different each week.

2. Try to encourage them and don't just look for them to encourage you.

Week 10: Sunday Worship
(I) Always need spiritual encouragement to endure.
(Therefore, I) Attend regular church meetings.

- Open up with a word of prayer.
- How are you doing? How's life?
- Share about your life. Model openness and seek their input.
- How were your Q.T.'s? Prayer life? Consistency is key.
- Let's review this week's quiet times together.

Can you quote the memory verse? Ephesians 2:19-20.
As you review the quiet times from the past week:
1) Reread the main scripture for each day of the week together.
2) How did this verse relate to the theme of the week?
3) How did you feel this verse applied to you personally?

> **Review Monday:** Read 1 Corinthians 11:23-26.
> **Review Tuesday:** Read 1 Corinthians 16:1-3.
> **Review Wednesday:** Read James 5:16.
> **Review Thursday:** Read Ephesians 5:17-21.
> **Review Friday:** Read Ephesians 4:11-16.

Conclusion:

Our unity as a church is supposed to be a testament to the world that we come from God (John 17:21). Many people in the world today have grown discouraged because of the disunity and confusion found in so-called Christianity. True believers are unified under the lordship of Christ. Jesus said that the Father seeks those who would worship him *in Spirit and in truth.* True worship involves not only sincerity, but also truth. Jesus clarifies this statement by defining truth as God's Word (John 17:17).

Application:

Here are some practical suggestions:

1. As you read the New Testament letters, remember that you are seeing for yourself what the first-century church taught.

Week 11: Dying to Self and Living for Christ
(I) Let God's Word Guide my Life.
(Therefore, I) Biblically Memorize and Meditate.

- Open up with a word of prayer.
- How are you doing? How's life?
- Share about your life. Model openness and seek their input.
- How were your Q.T.'s? Prayer life? Consistency is key.
- Let's review this week's quiet times together.

Can you quote the memory verse? Luke 9:23.
As you review the quiet times from the past week:
1. Reread the main scripture for each day of the week.
2. How did this verse relate to the theme of the week?
3. How did you feel this verse applied to you personally?

Review Monday: Read Luke 9:57-62.
Review Tuesday: Read Philippians 3:7-8.
Review Wednesday: Read Ephesians 4:22-24.
Review Thursday: Read Luke 9:23-27.
Review Friday: Read Philippians 3:12-14.

Conclusion:

Becoming a Christian requires a renewing of the mind and death to one's old way of life. Romans 6:4 says, *"we were therefore buried with him through baptism into death in order that, just as Christ was raised from the dead through the glory of the Father, we too may live a new life."* Yet far too many Christians are allowing their old sinful life to control them. As disciples of Christ, we need to die to ourselves daily, and live for Christ.

Application:

Here are some practical suggestions:
1. In everything, ask yourself "Am I pleasing God?"
2. Ask God to help you to become more like Christ.

Week 12: *Should I Follow My Heart?*
(I) Let God's Word Guide my Life.
(Therefore, I) Biblically Memorize and Meditate.

- Open up with a word of prayer.
- How are you doing? How's life?
- Share about your life. Model openness and seek their input.
- How were your Q.T.'s? Prayer life? Consistency is key!
- Let's review this week's quiet times together.

Can you quote the memory verse? Jeremiah 17:9.
As you review the quiet times from the past week:
1. Reread the main scripture for each day of the week.
2. How did this verse relate to the theme of the week?
3. How did you feel this verse applied to you personally?

> **Review Monday:** Read 1 Samuel 16:7.
> **Review Tuesday:** Read Jeremiah 17:9-10.
> **Review Wednesday:** Read Hebrews 3:12-13.
> **Review Thursday:** Read Luke 8:15.
> **Review Friday:** Read 2 Chronicles 16:9.

Conclusion:
So many of us are used to following the desires of our hearts, which change constantly. God calls us to follow the desires of his heart, which never change. You can find the desires of God's heart in his Word. Strive to gain greater self-control over your feeling and based your decisions on the Word and not your heart.

Application:
Here are some practical suggestions:
1. Pray for a pure heart.
2. Confess sin and be humble.

Week 13: *Let Others Help You*
(I) Understand my need for godly training.
(Therefore, I) Invite discipling in my life.

- Open up with a word of prayer.
- How are you doing? How's life?
- Share about your life. Model openness and seek their input.
- How were your Q.T.'s? Prayer life? Consistency is key.
- Let's review this week's quiet times together.

Can you quote the memory verse? Proverbs 27:17.
As you review the quiet times from the past week:
  1. Reread the main scripture for each day of the week.
  2. How did this verse relate to the theme of the week?
  3. How did you feel this verse applied to you personally?

> **Review Monday:** Read Jeremiah 18:2-6.
> **Review Tuesday:** Read Psalm 141:5.
> **Review Wednesday:** Read Hebrews 5:7-9.
> **Review Thursday:** Read 2 Corinthians 7:10-11.
> **Review Friday:** Read 1 Peter 5:5-9.

Conclusion:

Being molded after the likeness of the Lord should be every Christian's focus. To be like Jesus in every way is the attitude and desire of every true believer. Jesus calls us to be his disciples. But this requires a special kind of heart—a willing and moldable heart that is pliable like soft clay. Our mind-set and response to discipline will determine the kind of "vessel" we will become. What type of clay are you? Moldable, or rigid and unyielding?

Application:

Here are some practical suggestions:

  1. Ask those who are closest to you what they think you could grow in. Do not defend yourself, but rather listen and ask yourself, "How do I think I can change that?"

Week 14: Rabbi Jesus and Discipleship
(I) Understand my need for godly training.
(Therefore, I) Invite discipling in my life.

- Open up with a word of prayer.
- How are you doing? How's life?
- Share about your life. Model openness and seek their input.
- How were your Q.T.'s? Prayer life? Consistency is key.
- Let's review this week's quiet times together.

Can you quote the memory verse? James 5:16.
As you review the quiet times from the past week:
1. Reread the main scripture for each day of the week.
2. How did this verse relate to the theme of the week?
3. How did you feel this verse applied to you personally?

Review Monday: Read Matthew 28:18-20.
Review Tuesday: Read Hebrews 4:12-13.
Review Wednesday: Read Ezekiel 33:7-11.
Review Thursday: Read Romans 14:12-13.
Review Friday: Read Hebrews 12:5-16.

Conclusion:

If we want to stay faithful till the end we need to make sure we are doing the things that will keep us faithful. Accountability is all about being responsible for the things that God wants us to do. We are accountable to God, his Word, his church and to ourselves.

Application:

Hear are some practical suggestions:
1. Just remember that accountability isn't about people telling you what to do, but rather it's about making sure you are doing the things that are necessary to stay faithful to God and his Word.

Week 15: Sharing My Faith
(I) Enjoy bringing souls to Christ.
(Therefore, I) Tell others the good news.

- Open up with a word of prayer.
- How are you doing? How's life?
- Share about your life. Model openness and seek their input.
- How were your Q.T.'s? Prayer life? Consistency is key.
- Let's review this week's quiet times together.

Can you quote the memory verse? Philemon 6.

As you review the quiet times from the past week:
1. Reread the main scripture for each day of the week together.
2. How did this verse relate to the theme of the week?
3. How did you feel this verse applied to you personally?

> **Review Monday:** Read 2 Corinthians 5:10-21.
> **Review Tuesday:** Read Matthew 28:18-20.
> **Review Wednesday:** Read Romans 1:16-17.
> **Review Thursday:** Read 1 Peter 3:15-16.
> **Review Friday:** Read 1 Corinthians 9:20-23.

Conclusion:

Evangelism requires us to be both bold and tactful. Many Christians go from one extreme to the other. They are so tactful that they say little or nothing, while others may be so bold that tact is thrown out the window. As disciples of Christ, we need to pray for boldness in preaching the gospel (Ephesians 6:19). We also need to let our conversation be full of grace (Colossians 4:6).

Application:

Here are some practical suggestions:
1. Make a one a day challenge. Strive to share your faith with at least one person everyday. Start with those you know.

Week 16: Proclaiming Christ
(I) Enjoy bringing souls to Christ.
(Therefore, I) Tell others the good news.

- Open up with a word of prayer.
- How are you doing? How's life?
- Share about your life. Model openness and seek their input.
- How were your Q.T.'s? Prayer life? Consistency is key.
- Let's review this week's quiet times together.

Can you quote the memory verse? Matthew 28:19-20.

As you review the quiet times from the past week:
1. Reread the main scripture for each day of the week together.
2. How did this verse relate to the theme of the week?
3. How did you feel this verse applied to you personally?

Review Monday: Read Matthew 10:32-33.
Review Tuesday: Read Mark 5:18-20.
Review Wednesday: Read Acts 24:24-25.
Review Thursday: Read Psalm 145:8-12.
Review Friday: Read 1 Peter 3:15.

Conclusion:

Any time an artist creates a masterpiece it reflects the brilliance of his creativity and skill. Likewise, our lives proclaim the glory of God. The more like Jesus we become the more our very lives will draw people to God.

Application:

Here are some practical suggestions:

1. **Carry church invites with you.** Keep a fresh supply of church cards with your name, number, and church information on them. Invite people to service daily.

Week 17: *The Greatest in the Kingdom*
(I) Sincerely care about the needs of others.
(Therefore, I) Serve others with my S.H.A.P.E.

- Open up with a word of prayer.
- How are you doing? How's life?
- Share about your life. Model openness and seek their input.
- How were your Q.T.'s? Prayer life? Consistency is key.
- Let's review this week's quiet times together.

Can you quote the memory verse? Mark 10:45.

As you review the quiet times from the past week:
1. Reread the main scripture for each day of the week.
2. How did this verse relate to the theme of the week?
3. How did you feel this verse applied to you personally?

> **Review Monday:** Read Matthew 20:25-28.
> **Review Tuesday:** Read Colossians 3:23-24.
> **Review Wednesday:** Read Philippians 2:3-8.
> **Review Thursday:** Read Luke 17:7-10.
> **Review Friday:** Read John 13:12-17.

Conclusion:

God has completely different priorities than the world does. In God's eyes the greater the servant you are the greater you are in his eyes. In fact, those who God views as first in the kingdom are those who are slaves to others around them and slaves to the will of God.

Application:

Here are some practical suggestions:

1. Whenever you see a brother or a sister in need, offer to help. Contribute to others' needs (Romans 12:13).

2. When you serve, do it with a willing spirit *and* a smile.

Week 18: Let Your Light Shine

(I) Sincerely care about the needs of others.
(Therefore, I) Serve others with my S.H.A.P.E.

- Open up with a word of prayer.
- How are you doing? How's life?
- Share about your life. Model openness and seek their input.
- How were your Q.T.'s? Prayer life? Consistency is key.
- Let's review this week's quiet times together.

Can you quote the memory verse? Ephesians 2:10.

As you review the quiet times from the past week:
1. Reread the main scripture for each day of the week.
2. How did this verse relate to the theme of the week?
3. How did you feel this verse applied to you personally?

> **Review Monday:** Read Ephesians 2:10.
> **Review Tuesday:** Read Mark 10:45.
> **Review Wednesday:** Read 2 Corinthians 4:5.
> **Review Thursday:** Read John 13:34-35.
> **Review Friday:** Read Matthew 5:14-15.

Conclusion:

God has a purpose for our lives. We are not an accident. You have been SHAPE'd like no other and God wants to you your uniqueness to bring him glory!

Application:

Here are some practical suggestions:

1. **Ask God for Appointments.** God sets up works for you in advance to do. Pray that God will help your see those appointments and make the most of them.

Now that they've learned the V.A.L.U.E.S. & H.A.B.I.T.S. of a growing disciple it's important for them to immerse themselves into God's Word and see for themselves how Jesus and his disciples taught and lived those values and habits throughout the New Testament. The following is a schedule to read the entire New Testament in less than three months by taking 15-20 minutes a day and reading on average three chapters a day for 90 days.

The 6 Quick Tips focused on:

1. Begin by praying for God's help and end your reading by praying the **A.C.T.S.**
2. Don't worry about understanding and remembering everything you read.
3. At the end of each chapter write in a notebook what you think is the big idea.
4. If you have any questions write them down and ask an older disciple at a later time.
5. Write down how you think today's reading can help you in your new values and habits.
6. Pick one verse each week from your reading to memorize and meditate on.

Allow the next several weeks of your time together be dictated by the content of the scriptures they are reading. If there are any major issues or struggles always feel free to divert from the reading and address the issue going on. Find a scripture or two that they already know from their reading that has made an impact in your own life. Share those verses with them and how they have helped you in your walk with Christ.

Tips for making the most of your time together.

1) Open with the usual: Prayer, How's Life?, Did you do the reading?, etc.

2) Review the questions and thoughts they wrote down in their notebook.

    a. What stood out the most during your readings this week?

        i. How is that bringing you closer to God? How is that changing your life?

    b. What verse did you pick to memorize and meditate on? Can you quote it?

    c. Did you write down any questions you had about the scriptures you read?

        i. If you don't know the answer to their question be humble and tell them you'll study it out yourself, or ask someone else and get back to them.

3) What V.A.L.U.E.S. & H.A.B.I.T.S. did you see in your reading this week?

    a. How have you grown in that value or habit this week?

Week 19	Matthew 1-22
Week 20	Matthew 23-28, Acts 1-15
Week 21	Acts 16-28, Mark 1-9
Week 22	Mark 10-16, 1&2 Peter, James
Week 23	Luke 1-21
Week 24	Luke 22-24, 1&2 Thessalonians, 1 Corinthians 1-11
Week 25	1 Corinthians 12-16, 2 Corinthians, Revelation 1-3
Week 26	Revelation 4-22, Romans 1-3
Week 27	Romans 4-16, Galatians 1-4
Week 28	Galatians 5-6, Ephesians, Philippians, Colossians
Week 29	Philemon, Hebrews, 1 Timothy 1-3
Week 30	1 Timothy 4-6
Week 31	2 Timothy, Titus 1-3 2, John 1-12
Week 32	John 13-21, 1, 2&3 John, Jude

Week 33: *God Above All*

(I) Value my relationship w/ God, above all.
(Therefore, I) Have a Daily Quiet Time.

- Open up with a word of prayer.
- How are you doing? How's life?
- Share about your life. Model openness and seek their input.
- How were your Q.T.'s? Prayer life? Consistency is key.
- Let's review this week's quiet times together.

Can you quote the memory verse? Matthew 6:33.
As you review the quiet times from the past week:
1. Reread the main scripture for each day of the week.
2. How did this verse relate to the theme of the week?
3. How did you feel this verse applied to you personally?

Review Monday: Read Matthew 22:37-38.
Review Tuesday: Read Philippians 3:8-9.
Review Wednesday: Read 2 Chronicles 16:6-13.
Review Thursday: Read Luke 14:25-35.
Review Friday: Read Hebrews 12:18-29.

Conclusion:

It is so important that you continue to share your heart for God with them. God has blessed us all in so many ways with his love, mercy, and grace that we can't even begin to count the ways. When we remember even a fraction of how amazing God has been to us then it seems almost crazy to imagine putting anything before him. God is worth all our love and devotion.

Application:

Here are some practical suggestions:

1. **Count your many blessings.** There's a great song that says, "Count your many blessings name them one by one. Count your many blessing see what God hath done."

Week 34: Living to Please God
(I) Value my relationship w/ God, above all.
(Therefore, I) Have a Daily Quiet Time.

- Open up with a word of prayer.
- How are you doing? How's life?
- Share about your life. Model openness and seek their input.
- How were your Q.T.s? Prayer life? Consistency is key.
- Let's review this week's quiet times together.

Can you quote the memory verse? 2 Corinthians 5:9.
As you review the quiet times from the past week:
1. Reread the main scripture for each day of the week.
2. How did this verse relate to the theme of the week?
3. How did you feel this verse applied to you personally?

Review Monday: Read John 4:34-38.
Review Tuesday: Read Mark 14:32-36.
Review Wednesday: Read Ephesians 5:15-21.
Review Thursday: Read James 4:13-17.
Review Friday: Read 1 Thessalonians 4:1-5.

Conclusion:

As children of God, we are called to live a life centered on pleasing God. The jobs we take, the work that we do, the things that we say, the things we ask for, and the reasons why we do should all be for the sake of Christ and to the glory of God. The design of the gospel was not only to teach us what we should believe, but also how we should walk. The Christian's life is not a walk of the flesh, but rather a walk in the Spirit. In all you do, let it be done to the glory of God.

Application:

Here are some practical suggestions:

1. **Let God be in all your decisions!** Ask yourself, "What would Jesus do?" or "What would be pleasing to God?"

Week 35: Building Others Up

(I) Always need spiritual encouragement to endure.
(Therefore, I) Attend regular church meetings.

- Open up with a word of prayer.
- How are you doing? How's life?
- Share about your life. Model openness and seek their input.
- How were your Q.T.'s? Prayer life? Consistency is key.
- Let's review this week's quiet times together.

Can you quote the memory verse? Proverbs 11:25.
As you review the quiet times from the past week:
1. Reread the main scripture for each day of the week.
2. How did this verse relate to the theme of the week?
3. How did you feel this verse applied to you personally?

Review Monday: Read Ephesians 4:11-13.
Review Tuesday: Read Ephesians 4:22-27.
Review Wednesday: Read Ephesians 4:29-32.
Review Thursday: Read Hebrews 6:7-8.
Review Friday: Read Ephesians 5:1-4.

Conclusion:

Could you image what the church and the world would be like if everyone spoke to each other only based on what they needed? Not on what we personally want, or to vent because we are upset, but what the other person needed. The world has yet to see how amazing life could be if a group of people would be solely devoted to building others up.

Application:

Here are some practical suggestions:

1. **Greet** your brother or sister with a loving hug! Hug visitors too. For there is no law against hugging.

2. **Invite** brothers and sisters into your home, especially those who you do not know you well (Romans 12:13b).

Week 36: *Appreciating Our Differences*
(I) Always need spiritual encouragement to endure.
(Therefore, I) Attend regular church meetings.

- Open up with a word of prayer.
- How are you doing? How's life?
- Share about your life. Model openness and seek their input.
- How were your Q.T.'s? Prayer life? Consistency is key.
- Let's review this week's quiet times together.

Can you quote the memory verse? Ephesians 4:2-3.
As you review the quiet times from the past week:
1. Reread the main scripture for each day of the week.
2. How did this verse relate to the theme of the week?
3. How did you feel this verse applied to you personally?

> **Review Monday:** Read Matthew 13:47-52.
> **Review Tuesday:** Read Acts 10:34.
> **Review Wednesday:** Read Galatians 2:11-16
> **Review Thursday:** Read Romans 12:4-8.
> **Review Friday:** Read 1 Corinthians 1:26-ff.

Conclusion:
By understanding that your S.H.A.P.E. is unique, and that you are only part of a team (Ephesians 4:16) you will appreciate the strengths that others bring in building up the kingdom.

Application:

Here are some practical suggestions:

1. **Discover their S.H.A.P.E.** Ask other disciples what their SHAPE is in order to get to know them better.

Week 37: Living Faith
(I) Let God's Word Guide my Life.
(Therefore, I) Biblically Memorize and Meditate.

- Open up with a word of prayer.
- How are you doing? How's life?
- Share about your life. Model openness and seek their input.
- How were your Q.T.'s? Prayer life? Consistency is key.
- Let's review this week's quiet times together.

Can you quote the memory verse? James 2:22.
As you review the quiet times from the past week:
1. Reread the main scripture for each day of the week.
2. How did this verse relate to the theme of the week?
3. How did you feel this verse applied to you personally?

> **Review Monday:** Read Ecclesiastes 7:15-18.
> **Review Tuesday:** Read James 2:14-26.
> **Review Wednesday:** Read Ephesians 2:8-10.
> **Review Thursday:** Read Titus 3:5-7.
> **Review Friday:** Read Jude 4.

Conclusion:

The road of salvation is not traveled by works. As disciples of Jesus Christ, we need to realize that to depend on our good deeds for salvation is foolish and worthless. It is only through Jesus' death on the cross that we are saved. It is equally sad, however, when some people talk about grace so much that they truly use it as a license to either sin or be lukewarm in their commitment to Christ.

Application:

Here are some practical suggestions:

1. Think of one thing you know you should do, but don't do consistently and be determined to live it out from now on.

Week 38: Obey God's Commands
(I) Let God's Word Guide my Life.
(Therefore, I) Biblically Memorize and Meditate.

- Open up with a word of prayer.
- How are you doing? How's life?
- Share about your life. Model openness and seek their input.
- How were your Q.T.'s? Prayer life? Consistency is key.
- Let's review this week's quiet times together.

Can you quote the memory verse? Luke 6:46.
As you review the quiet times from the past week:
1. Reread the main scripture for each day of the week.
2. How did this verse relate to the theme of the week?
3. How did you feel this verse applied to you personally?

Review Monday: Read Ephesians 5:22-27.
Review Tuesday: Read Matthew 7:21-23.
Review Wednesday: Read 1 Peter 1:22-23.
Review Thursday: Read 1 Peter 1:14-25.
Review Friday: Read Exodus 20.

Conclusion:

Our goal must be to stop trying to obey God in order to get to Heaven, but rather obey God because we are going to Heaven. Obey God because you trust that his commands truly are designed to give you God's absolute best. This type of obedience is an absolute joy!

Application:
Here are some practical suggestions:

1. **Pray daily to God.** Be open about the areas in your life that need to change. Ask for wisdom and willingness on your part to allow God to change you.

2. **Let God communicate with you.** Read the Word as if God is speaking directly with you because he is. Take what you read as his advice, and personally apply it to your life.

Week 39: A Disciplined Life
(I) Understand my need for godly training.
(Therefore, I) Invite discipling in my life.

- Open up with a word of prayer.
- How are you doing? How's life?
- Share about your life. Model openness and seek their input.
- How were your Q.T.'s? Prayer life? Consistency is key.
- Let's review this week's quiet times together.

Can you quote the memory verse? 1 Timothy 4:7.
As you review the quiet times from the past week:
1. Reread the main scripture for each day of the week.
2. How did this verse relate to the theme of the week?
3. How did you feel this verse applied to you personally?

> **Review Monday:** Read 1 Tim. 4:7-11.
> **Review Tuesday:** Read Hebrews 6:11-12.
> **Review Wednesday:** Read 1 Thessalonians 4:11-12.
> **Review Thursday:** Read 2 Thessalonians 3:6-15.
> **Review Friday:** Read Hebrews 12:11-15.

Conclusion:
Few, if any of us, are naturally disciplined. Discipline must be learned. Without discipline we will not be able to take the world for Christ. Discipline must be built into our Christian lives from the earliest possible moment. Christ came to the world to save the world (John 3:17). He came for a people eager to do what is good (Titus 2:14); Workers for the kingdom of God. Are you a worker for the Lord?

Application:
Here are some practical suggestions:
1. Learn to keep a calendar and a to-do list.
2. Spend time with a disciplined person and follow his or her example.

Possess these qualities in increasing measure...and you will never fall!

Week 40: *Valuing One Another*
(I) Understand my need for godly training.
(Therefore, I) Invite discipling in my life.

- Open up with a word of prayer.
- How are you doing? How's life?
- Share about your life. Model openness and seek their input.
- How were your Q.T.'s? Prayer life? Consistency is key.
- Let's review this week's quiet times together.

Can you quote the memory verse? Philippians 2:3-4.
As you review the quiet times from the past week:
1. Reread the main scripture for each day of the week.
2. How did this verse relate to the theme of the week?
3. How did you feel this verse applied to you personally?

Review Monday: Read 1 Peter 2:9-ff.
Review Tuesday: Read Colossians 3:12-14.
Review Wednesday: Read Ephesians 4:29-ff.
Review Thursday: Read Proverbs 18:19-21.
Review Friday: Read Philippians 2:1-4.

Conclusion:

Remember the Lord's command: *"...Love one another. As I have loved you...By this all men will know that you are my disciples..."* (John 13:34-35). Our love for God is displayed by the way we love and honor one another.

Application:
Here are some practical suggestions:

1. **Get to know one another.** Don't be satisfied with just knowing *about* your brother or sister; get to know them. Fellowship with them.

2. **Learn to listen!** When a brother or sister comes to you for advice or to talk, make sure you give them your full attention. Be ready to meet their spiritual needs.

Week 41: A Ministry of Reconciliation
(I) Enjoy bringing souls to Christ.
(Therefore, I) Tell others the good news.

- Open up with a word of prayer.
- How are you doing? How's life?
- Share about your life. Model openness and seek their input.
- How were your Q.T.'s? Prayer life? Consistency is key.
- Let's review this week's quiet times together.

Can you quote the memory verse? 2 Corinthians 5:20.
As you review the quiet times from the past week:
1. Reread the main scripture for each day of the week.
2. How did this verse relate to the theme of the week?
3. How did you feel this verse applied to you personally?

> **Review Monday:** Read 2 Cor. 5:17-21.
> **Review Tuesday:** Read 1 Corinthians 13:4-8.
> **Review Wednesday:** Read Romans 14:17-21.
> **Review Thursday:** Read Proverbs 18:19.
> **Review Friday:** Read Philippians 2:12-18.

Conclusion:
    We live in a broken world. The key to healing our broken lives is to start by healing our broken relationship with God. When you lead people back to Christ you are helping them experience the greatest act of healing in their lives. This involves helping others to be at peace with God by proclaiming the gospel of peace (Romans 5:1; Ephesians 6:15).

Application:
Here are some practical suggestions:
1. **One a day challenge.** Hopefully you have already tried to apply this to your life, but this is an amazing way to get your eyes to consistently looking for those who need to be reconciled to God.

Week 42: You Are the Salt of the Earth
(I) Enjoy bringing souls to Christ.
(Therefore, I) Tell others the good news.

- Open up with a word of prayer.
- How are you doing? How's life?
- Share about your life. Model openness and seek their input.
- How were your Q.T.'s? Prayer life? Consistency is key.
- Let's review this week's quiet times together.

Can you quote the memory verse? Matthew 5:13.
As you review the quiet times from the past week:
1. Reread the main scripture for each day of the week.
2. How did this verse relate to the theme of the week?
3. How did you feel this verse applied to you personally?

> **Review Monday:** Read Matthew 5:13.
> **Review Tuesday:** Read Romans 12:1-2.
> **Review Wednesday:** Read 2 Kings 2:20-21.
> **Review Thursday:** Read 2 Timothy 2:15.
> **Review Friday:** Read Mark 9:50.

Conclusion:

Christians are the salt of the earth. We are called to live lives that impact others where ever we go. We are called not only to teach the gospel, but to live lives worthy of the gospel (Colossians 1:10). Do your words and actions impact others in a powerful way for God's glory? Do men see Christ living in you? Are you the salt of the earth?

Application:

Here are some practical suggestions:

1. **Be a source of encouragement.** Be known as a person who edifies, both in the spiritual and secular realms. Learn to keep your joy when everyone else around you is stressed.

Week 43: *The Most Excellent Way*
(I) Sincerely care about the needs of others.
(Therefore, I) Serve others with my S.H.A.P.E.

- Open up with a word of prayer.
- How are you doing? How's life?
- Share about your life. Model openness and seek their input.
- How were your Q.T.'s? Prayer life? Consistency is key.
- Let's review this week's quiet times together.

Can you quote the memory verse? Mark 12:31.
As you review the quiet times from the past week:
1. Reread the main scripture for each day of the week.
2. How did this verse relate to the theme of the week?
3. How did you feel this verse applied to you personally?

Review Monday: Read Mark 12:28-34.
Review Tuesday: Read Deuteronomy 6:20-25.
Review Wednesday: Read Deuteronomy 10:12-ff.
Review Thursday: Read Deuteronomy 11:26-27.
Review Friday: Read Revelation 2:1-7.

Application:
Here are some helpful suggestions:

1. *Love the LORD with all your heart!* God put things in your heart that you are passionate about. Use those things to love God by using what he put in your heart.

2. *Love the LORD with all your soul!* Give your entire being to God to use in any way He desires.

3. *Love the LORD with all your mind!* You have experiences that God wants to use to bring comfort and training to others. Remember those experiences and share them.

4. *Love the LORD with all your strength!* Never give up serving the Lord. Do everything to the glory of Christ, your Lord (Colossians. 3:17).

Week 44: Use Your Gifts to Serve Others
(I) Sincerely care about the needs of others.
(Therefore, I) Serve others with my S.H.A.P.E.

- Open up with a word of prayer.
- How are you doing? How's life?
- Share about your life. Model openness and seek their input.
- How were your Q.T.'s? Prayer life? Consistency is key.
- Let's review this week's quiet times together.

Can you quote the memory verse? Luke 12:48.
As you review the quiet times from the past week:
1. Reread the main scripture for each day of the week.
2. How did this verse relate to the theme of the week?
3. How did you feel this verse applied to you personally?

Review Monday: Read Luke 12:42-48.
Review Tuesday: Read Luke 19:12-27.
Review Wednesday: Read Matthew 25:14-30.
Review Thursday: Read Luke 8:4-15.
Review Friday: What do you remember from 2 Chronicles 34 and 35 and the story of Josiah?

Conclusion:

One of the greatest struggles many people have is acknowledging the gifts that God has given them (remember your S.H.A.P.E.). Realize how gifted you really are in Christ and how God expects you to prove faithful with them.

Application:

Hear are some practical suggestions:
1. Think about the blessings God has granted to you.
2. Make a list of them.
3. Next to each one write how you are worshipping God with this ability or gift (could be a material gift or possession).

Week 44: *Use Your Gifts to Serve Others*

Over the next several weeks the young disciple is going to spend time in the Old Testament looking at the heart and the wisdom of God. The goal is to focus on the practical's of everyday living as is found in the Proverbs, but also focus on the motivation of pleasing and praising God as is found in the Psalms.

The 6 Quick Tips focused on:

1. Begin by praying for God's help and end your reading by praying the A.C.T.S.
2. Don't worry about understanding and remembering everything you read.
3. At the end of each chapter write in a notebook what stood out to you the most.
4. If you have any questions write them down and ask an older disciple at a later time.
5. Write down how you think today's reading can help you in your new values and habits.
6. Pick one verse each week from your reading to memorize and meditate on.

Allow the next several weeks of your time together be dictated by the content of the scriptures they are reading. If there are any major issues or struggles always feel free to divert from the reading and address the issue going on.

Tips for making the most of your time together.

1) Open with the usual: Prayer, How's Life?, Did you do the reading?, etc.

2) Review the questions and thoughts they wrote down in their notebook.

a. What stood out the most during your readings this week?
   i. How is that bringing you closer to God? How is that changing your life?
b. What verse did you pick to memorize and meditate on? Can you quote it?
c. Did you write down any questions you had about the scriptures you read?
   i. If you don't know the answer to their question be humble and tell them you'll study it out yourself, ask someone else and get back to them.

3) What V.A.L.U.E.S. & H.A.B.I.T.S. did you see in your reading this week?
   a. How have you grown in that value or habit this week?

The readings in the Psalms are theme based.
Choose 1 or 2 themes to focus on during your time.

Week 45: Blessing, Calling to God, Confidence, Deeds of God, Doubt, Faithfulness of God and Fear.

Week 46: Glory of God, God is a Helper, Identity, Justice of God, Meditation, Mercy, Music.

Week 47: Nature, Peace, Power of God, Praise, Prayer, Protection, Safety in God.

Week 48: Rejoicing, Righteousness, Salvation, Sin and Repentance, Thanksgiving, Trust.

Week 49: Victory, Wisdom, Worship and Proverbs 1-4.

Week 50: Proverbs 5-12.

Week 51: Proverbs 13-20.

Week 52: Proverbs 21-27 (28-31 are still remaining). Encourage them to finish those three this week.

Recommended Reading

- *Foundations For Faith: Old Testament Survey.* Douglas Jacoby. Illumination Publishers. ISBN: 0-9767583-7-7.

- *The Faith Unfurled: New Testament Survey.* Douglas Jacoby. Illumination Publishers. ISBN: 0-9767583-4-2.

- *Shining Like Stars: An Evangelism Handbook.* Douglas Jacoby. Illumination Publishers. ISBN: 0-9776954-0-9.

- *The Spirit.* Douglas Jacoby. Illumination Publishers. ISBN: 0-9745342-8-5.

- *The Victory of Surrender.* Gordon Ferguson. DPI. ISBN: 1-57782-185-8.

- *Romans: The Heart Set Free.* Gordon Ferguson. DPI. ISBN: 1-5778216-8-8.

- *The Power of Discipling.* Gordon Ferguson. DPI. ISBN: 1-577821-53-X.

- *Prepared to Answer (Second Edition).* Gordon Ferguson. Illumination Publishers. ISBN: 978-0-9824085-06.

- *Love One Another.* Gordon Ferguson. DPI. ISBN: 1-884553-18-4.

- *Prideful Soul's Guide to Humility.* Tom Jones and Mike Fontenot. DPI. ISBN: 1-57782-186-6.

- *One Another.* Tom Jones/Steve Brown. DPI. ISBN: 978-1-57782-229-5.

- *The Lion Never Sleeps.* Mike Taliaferro. DPI. ISBN: 1-57782-184-X.

- *The Killer Within.* Mike Taliaferro. DPI. ISBN: 1-5778204-2-8.

- *That You May Believe.* Dr. John Oakes and David Eastman. Illumination Publishers. ISBN: 978-0-9797886-6-6.

- *From Shadow to Reality.* Dr. John Oakes. Illumination Publishers. ISBN: 0-9745342-3-4.

- *Is There a God?* Dr. John Oakes. Illumination Publishers. ISBN: 0-9776954-2-5.

- *How We Got the Bible and Why You Can Trust It.* Mike Taliaferro. Illumunation Publishers. ISBN: 978-0-9824085-2-0.

- *Raising Awesome Kids.* Sam and Geri Laing. DPI. ISBN: 978-1-57782-234-9.

- *The Quiver: Christian Parenting in a Non-Christian World.* Douglas and Vicki Jacoby. Illumination Publishers. ISBN: 0-9767583-6-9.

- *World Changers: The History of the Church in the Book of Acts.* Gordon Ferguson. Illumination Publishers. ISBN: 978-0-9839157-0-6.

- *Share Your Faith: Creative Ways to Help a Hurting World.* Steve Cannon and Eric Gaizat. Illumination Publishers. ISBN: 978-0-9835411-2-7.

Recommended Websites

- www.BryanGrayMinistries.com. *Teaching website of Bryan Gray.*

- www.ipibooks.com. *Books and Audio/Video from Illumination Publishers.*

- www.DisciplesToday.org. *Official website of the Intl. Churches of Christ.*

- www.DoesGodExist.org. *Apologetic website for John Clayton.*

- www.DouglasJacoby.com. *Teaching website of Dr. Douglas Jacoby.*

- www.gftm.org. *Teaching website of Gordon Ferguson.*

- www.BostonCoC.org. *The website of the Boston Church of Christ.*

- www.blueletterbible.org. *Resource site for Bible study.*

- www.Biblegateway.org. Resource site for Bible study.

- www.JimMcGuiggan.com. *Teaching ministry of Jim McGuiggan.*

- www.Change4God.com. *Teaching ministry of Steve Cannon.*

- www.EvidenceforChristianity.org. Teaching ministry of Dr. John M. Oakes.

- www.ICOCHotnews.com. *News from the Intl. Churches of Christ.*

Bryan Gray

For the latest news from the ministry of Bryan Gray go to his website. It is continually updated with articles, video and audio teaching.

Illumination Publishers International

Toney Mulhollan has worked in Christian publishing for 35 years. He has served as the Production Manager for Crossroads Publications, Discipleship Magazine/Upside Down Magazine, Discipleship Publications International (DPI) and on the production teams of Campus Journal, Biblical Discipleship Quarterly, Bible Illustrator and others.

Toney serves as Executive Editor of Illumination Publishers International. He is happily married to the love of his life, Denise L. Mulhollan, M.D. They make their home in Houston, Texas along with their daughters, Audra Joan and Cali Owen.

For the best in Christian writing and audio instruction, go to the Illumination Publishers website. We're committed to producing in depth teaching that will inform, inspire and encourage Christians to a deeper and more committed walk with God. You can e-mail us at our website below.

www.ipibooks.com

CPSIA information can be obtained at www.ICGtesting.com
Printed in the USA
BVOW08s0948110416

443607BV00001B/2/P